T0113990

# Cambridge Elements ≡

Elements in Publishing and Book Culture
edited by
Samantha Rayner
*University College London*
Leah Tether
*University of Bristol*

# TEACHING PUBLISHING AND EDITORIAL PRACTICE

## *The Transition from University to Industry*

Jocelyn Hargrave
*University of Melbourne*

**CAMBRIDGE**
UNIVERSITY PRESS

# CAMBRIDGE
## UNIVERSITY PRESS

University Printing House, Cambridge CB2 8BS, United Kingdom

One Liberty Plaza, 20th Floor, New York, NY 10006, USA

477 Williamstown Road, Port Melbourne, VIC 3207, Australia

314–321, 3rd Floor, Plot 3, Splendor Forum, Jasola District Centre,
New Delhi – 110025, India

103 Penang Road, #05–06/07, Visioncrest Commercial, Singapore 238467

Cambridge University Press is part of the University of Cambridge.

It furthers the University's mission by disseminating knowledge in the pursuit of
education, learning, and research at the highest international levels of excellence.

www.cambridge.org
Information on this title: www.cambridge.org/9781108791946
DOI: 10.1017/9781108866880

First published 2022

*A catalogue record for this publication is available from the British Library.*

ISBN 978-1-108-79194-6 Paperback
ISSN 2514-8524 (online)
ISSN 2514-8516 (print)

# Teaching Publishing and Editorial Practice

## The Transition from University to Industry

### Elements in Publishing and Book Culture

DOI: 10.1017/9781108866880

First published online: January 2022

Jocelyn Hargrave

*University of Melbourne*

Author for correspondence: Jocelyn Hargrave, jocelyn.hargrave@unimelb.edu.au

ABSTRACT: A key challenge facing all educators working in practice-based subjects is the need to negotiate tensions between past and present and provide training that prepares students for fast-changing conditions while also conveying long-standing principles. This Element therefore investigates how effectively editing and publishing programmes prepare graduates for industry and how well these graduates translate this instruction to the workplace. Taking a global perspective to gauge the state of the discipline, the mixed-methods approach used for this Element comprised two online surveys for educators and graduates, three semi-structured interviews with industry practitioners (scholarly, education and trade) and ethnographic practice (author as educator and practitioner). Three key concepts also framed this Element's enquiry: being, learning and doing. The Element demonstrates how these transitioning but interdependent concepts have the potential to form a holistic practice-led pedagogy for students of editing and publishing programmes.

KEYWORDS: editorial pedagogy, editorial practice, publishing, graduates, transition

ISBNs: 9781108791946 (PB), 9781108866880 (OC)

ISSNs: 2514-8524 (online), 2514-8516 (print)

# Contents

# 1 Introduction

This book looks at editing and publishing programmes in higher education as a specific sector that yields important insights with broader applicability. In particular, it investigates how effectively such programmes prepare graduates for industry and how well these graduates translate this instruction in the workplace. Such an enquiry throws light on a key challenge facing all educators working in practice-based subjects: the need to negotiate tensions between past and present and provide training that prepares students for fast-changing conditions while also conveying long-standing principles. As Albers and Flanagan (2019, p. 3) observe, 'the quality of the courses determines how well students adjust to editing in the workplace and how much time practitioners need to invest in training new employees'. To gauge the state of the discipline, this book takes an international perspective; programmes and their graduates in the following countries were approached to contribute: Australia, Canada, England, Germany, India, New Zealand, Scotland, South Africa and the United States.

This study's research questions pertain to how educators have developed editorial pedagogy for the higher-education sector, particularly in response to ongoing digital disruption of the publishing industry:

- How effectively do the programmes negotiate theory and practice.
- How have students perceived these programmes to be suitable for, or even reflective of, contemporary practice.
- In what ways do these programmes prepare graduates for the workplace – that is, did graduates develop the requisite industry skills at university, and which did they develop 'on the job'.
- How do graduates believe these programmes can be improved, if necessary, to better prepare them for industry.

Nevertheless, this book recognises that it is unrealistic, even unreasonable, to perceive universities as a one-stop shop: 'no program [sic] can ever be agile enough to keep up with every new trend in industry' (Melonçon 2019, p. 179). This is particularly the case when technological developments tend to outpace educators' own skills acquisition and their administrative – as well as political – capacity to build these into established pedagogy. In turn, it is vital that the publishing industry understands this reality: that administrative, financial and political capacity of universities complicates their appropriate response to market requirements and expectations. Ciofalo (1988, p. 4) was an early witness to such constraints or 'territorial tug of war' (Kruger 2007, p. 3):[1]

> The college needs to respond to industry representations concerning requisite skills and course configurations to prepare college graduates for careers in book publishing. And the industry needs to be realistic about the limitations, economic and pedagogical, of the college in meeting professional needs within a liberal arts format. There's a 'quid pro quo' here.

It remains necessary, however, to assess the effectiveness of university programmes as little research appears to have been undertaken, especially from students' perspectives. This paucity of research has been acknowledged by Chavan et al. (2014, p. 151):

> [S]tudents' perceptions of the quality of the educational services that they are receiving have deep psychological underpinnings and are more multidimensional in nature ... to date, little is understood about students' perceptions of the quality of service that they are receiving, and how this influences not only the nature of the student experience, but also important marketing outcomes for the tertiary sector such as student satisfaction, recommendation and loyalty.

This book therefore intends to fill the research gap, and in so doing, three key concepts frame the enquiry: *being*, *learning* and *doing*. These

---

[1]  According to Kruger (2007, p. 3), 'academia is trying to claim a discipline that has not traditionally been academic, while the publishing industry remains protective of a field that it feels can only be mastered adequately in the "real world"'.

transitioning but interdependent concepts have the potential to form a holistic practice-led pedagogy for students of editing and publishing programmes.

## *Being: An Editorial (and Publishing) Ontology*

A study of literature published on pedagogy and editorial practice uncovers several common debates and dichotomies: the need for more distinct nomenclature to define editors and editorial practice, nature versus nurture and the requisite personal and professional attributes to be a 'good' editor. Such consideration is also applicable to publishing generally.

### Nomenclature to Define Editors and Editorial Practice

This section on nomenclature concentrates on defining in more precise terms not *who* editors are – namely their ideal, assumed and/or true attributes (to be considered later in this 'Being' section) – but *what* they are and *how* they perform – that is, their editorial practice. The application of the term *nomenclature* here as a quantifying framework was inspired by Fretz (2017, p. 246), who insightfully explains that:

> unless a single person performs all functions in the publishing workflow, multiple people need to be involved in producing a book or journal. For these various people to share the same understanding of the editorial work involved, they need to be able to communicate their assumptions and expectations clearly to one another. Clear communication depends on shared nomenclature, clear definitions of the terms being used, and a common understanding of the tasks associated with those terms.

In industry, assumptions and expectations are expressed not only from top to bottom (such as from managing editor to in-house and/or freelance editors) but also interdepartmentally (including design, production, permissions, sales and marketing and distribution) and with external stakeholders (who are either freelance, such as proofreaders and indexers, or from offshore, such as typesetters and printers). For academia, according to

Haugen (1990, p. 323),[2] the terminologies of researchers, such as those that focus on composition, have been inconsistent not just among themselves but also with industry:

> Book publishers have been using the term editing for about 200 years, and as publishers began relinquishing editing duties to persons other than themselves, the terms editing and its associated, product-based terms migrated into the professional editing arena. These product-based terms, certainly handy and ready to use, at the same time lacked the kinds of precision researchers would prefer. Some researchers, struggling with these problems, coined their own terms for what they were describing: recasting, reseeing, reconceiving. As a result, these various terms, both the old ones and the new ones, have been used inconsistently from study to study, and sometimes even within the same study.

Flanagan (2019, p. 20) has similarly witnessed the inconsistency more recently among technical communicators: 'They seem to agree that editing is a process, but the process may be defined in terms of technology, rhetoric, actors, activities, and/or disciplines'. Such inconsistencies and lack of standardisation have hindered educators' capacity to connect theory and practice – this is in evidence today, albeit to a lesser extent than that demonstrated by Haugen (1990). This conclusion also points to a paucity of research into editing courses themselves, particularly specialised editing (Albers and Flanagan 2019, p. 2). The nomenclature therefore produced next constitutes the shared vocabulary and editorial understanding for this study – it seeks to connect industry with academia.

---

[2] Haugen's observations form part of a long-standing critique: years earlier, Ciofalo (1988, p. 3) observed, and advocated, the following: 'Too often higher education for the professions is undertaken with little dialogue exchanged between the institution and the industry it purports to service. Instead, there should be a deep and meaningful connection'.

The *Oxford English Dictionary* (*OED*) defines *editor*, in the second instance,[3] as '[a] person who prepares an edition of written work by one or more authors for publication, by selecting and arranging the contents, adding commentary'. The term *editor* appears therefore to be derived literally from *edition*, which is defined as 'one of the forms in which a work is published and issued at one point in time' (Hall 2013, p. 180). This definition of *editor* for the modern context, however, pertains particularly to scholarly editors who prepare critical editions of, for example, classical, historical and literary texts. Greenberg (2018, p. 184) observes that scholarly editing is 'sometimes described as . . . post-publication editing' (see also Kruger 2007, p. 6).

For the publishing industry, the *OED*'s third entry is relevant, though complex in nature: 'a person who edits written material for publication or use; one who selects, assesses, or commissions material for publication or broadcast'. The *OED*'s third entry is complex in nature because it refers to two types, or occupations, of editor: the second half of the entry relates to commissioning or developmental editors who are 'responsible for coming up with marketable ideas and matching them to good authors' (Clark and Phillips 2019, p. 156), and the first to copy editors who 'edit copy for printing' – that is, manuscripts. Manuscript editors are often also termed copy editors, line editors or desk editors (Poland 2007, p. 100). Hall (2013, p. 180) insightfully observes the key difference between commissioning and manuscript editors: '[Editorial] tasks can essentially crystalize [sic] around two core functions: first that of commissioning – the "what" of writing; and second that of correcting, smoothing, and rewriting text – the "how" of writing'. Hence, the *how* of editorial practice embodies the central focus of this book.

The *how* does not comprise only 'correcting, smoothing and rewriting', however. The fundamentals, as itemised by Butcher et al. (2006, pp. 1–2) and consistent with practising editors' reality, consist of substantive editing (improving 'the overall coverage and presentation

---

[3] The first definition, 'a publisher of a book', is identified as obsolete.

of a piece of writing, its content, scope, length, level and organization'), 'detailed editing for sense' (not just clarity and concision of language but also fact-checking for accuracy), 'checking for consistency' (which can also be identified during the substantive edit) and providing 'clear presentation of the material for the typesetter' (such as the correct placement of photographs, tables and content to be inserted into margins). Interestingly, Einsohn (2011b, p. 11) stipulates the activities that manuscript editors are not expected to perform: ghostwriting, developmental editing, proofreading and designing publications. Manuscript editors collaborate with numerous stakeholders, such as authors, publishers, designers, typesetters, illustrators, production, permissions and freelance proofreaders and indexers, to bring titles to fruition, either in print or online; the demarcation between these stakeholders in the twenty-first-century publishing house is very distinct. As Poland (2007, pp. 101–102) explains, 'editors undertake three main tasks: structural editing, copy-editing and reviewing proof corrections. Together with book design, and production, these editorial processes may be regarded as key steps in a value-adding chain'.

The manner in which the fundamentals are executed is typically determined by both the sectors in which editors work and the manuscript copy itself. Ileene Smith related in her interview with Greenberg (2015, p. 50) her transition from a university publisher to the trade press Farrar, Straus and Giroux (FSG):

> It was also highly procedural, and that took some getting used to. In a university press there are publications committees and acquisitions panels and all kinds of things like that, which were new to me. There were sometimes very good things that resulted from these procedures but university presses don't tend to be as editorially driven as trade presses. This house – FSG – is very, very editorially driven.

In terms of content, for example, editors in the educational publishing industry tend to project, manage and/or edit highly complex and illustrative manuscripts, frequently written by multi-author teams and according to specific curricula. The complexity of editing these manuscripts is exacerbated by manuscript length; for example, tertiary texts often comprise 800–1,000 pages once typeset (Donoughue 2007, p. 212). Typical editorial responsibilities include completing manuscript appraisals to assess the structure, content and presentation of unedited manuscripts (substantive editing); ensuring page extent, budgets and schedules are maintained; editing and styling manuscripts on-screen (copy-editing for spelling, grammar, punctuation, style, consistency and accuracy); compiling artwork and permissions lists and editing artwork and photographic and text briefs; approving commissioned artwork; liaising with publishers, permissions, production, in-house editors and managing editors, authors and freelance proofreaders and indexers; marking up (i.e. correcting or annotating) typeset pages by hand or, most often, on-screen (Hargrave 2014, p. 213); and amalgamating the corrections of authors, publishers and proofreaders into an editorial master set to be forwarded to production. This inventory reveals the diverse administrative tasks that editors in the educational publishing industry are required to complete, in addition to the manuscript edit.

The present reality, particularly for in-house editors, is that the 'percentage of the workday spent on [editing] has greatly decreased' (Albers and Flanagan 2019, p. 3) because of the twenty-first-century gig economy's preference for hiring contract and freelance staff to limit project costs. Nevertheless, all editors are expected to perform these tasks whenever necessary and more according to the digital environment in which they work, with minimal supervision and financial outlay. According to Karen Lee (2019, p. 17), chief executive officer of the Institute of Professional Editors (IPEd), the national professional association for Australian editors:

> The editors of tomorrow will be digitally savvy communication consultants, coders, teachers, mentors and advocates for accessibility and inclusivity. Novels, textbooks, government reports, corporate documents, self-published books, scripts, social media, mainstream media, websites, apps, blogs, marketing materials and more – editors' skills will make them shine.

## Nature versus Nurture

Einsohn (2004, 2011a) has regularly asked the questions: 'Are Editors Born or Made?' Are aspiring editors born with the necessary drive and aptitude to become competent editors and succeed in the publishing industry (or any other industry where they are able to use their editorial expertise)?[4] That is, are drive and aptitude innate to the self, or can they also be formally cultivated, with all individuals obtaining similar levels of proficiency? Einsohn (2011a, p. 1) uses the terms *native talent* and *teachability* when considering the two states and concludes that ability can be taught but cannot be achieved for every individual who seeks to be an editor: 'No scientist has identified an editorial gene, and we have no documented reports of the muse Redactia visiting babies in their bassinets. Yet some people do seem better suited to editorial work than others'. Einsohn's conclusions agree with those previously given by Upton and Maner (1997, p. 2): 'Many [editorial attributes] can be enhanced and developed by training and experience, but a good editor will come to his or her profession with the kernel of these skills present and will build upon innate abilities'; as well as by Targ (1985, pp. 13–14): 'A working, qualified editor of books must read. He must have read from the earliest days of his childhood. His reading must be unceasing. The lust for printed matter is a biological thing, a visceral and intellectual necessity; the urge must be in the genes'. Indeed, for Targ, becoming an editor amounts to a 'calling' (p. 3) – it is more than an occupation but an editor's 'fate' (p. 20).

Nevertheless, Einsohn (2011a, p. 3) cautions with the caveat that the romantic 'love to read' sentiment is not a sufficient innate prerequisite that leads naturally to becoming a capable editor. This sentiment does appear to be a consistent starting point though if one looks at the career profiles of established professionals published in industry journals. For Australian editor and fiction writer Glenys Osborne (2009, p. 14), '[It] started with

---

[4] Albers and Flanagan (2019, p. 11) believe the 'title of "editor" is highly endangered. Although the editor is disappearing from the corporate workspace, the editing still happens. Each writer becomes a writer/editor working with the other members of their group. Or they work as a writer on one project and are charged with editing another'.

a book … The sensation of connecting with another's experience affected me profoundly. I think that's where I became both a passionate reader and a try-hard, would-be writer'. At sixteen, Osborne obtained her first position in the publishing industry as a proofreader's assistant. Robert Watkins (2013, p. 11), who climbed from account manager to head of literary and head of illustrated at Hachette Australia Books, narrated his precocious beginnings in a similarly nostalgic fashion: 'Ever since I was a young boy I could always be found with a book in hand. So it made sense, at the age of 16, to apply for a job at a bookstore'. Returning to Einsohn's (2011a) caveat, it seems that although an innate 'calling' is not a prerequisite, the innate drive to be an editor is without doubt beneficial as success within the profession requires stamina to respond to, and survive, editing's highly meticulous, administrative albeit rewarding nature.

## Attributes of a 'Good' Editor

People have enumerated, and judged, the attributes of a 'good' editor for hundreds of years with consistent agreement. In *Orthotypographia*, the first trade manual for editors and published in Leipzig in 1608, Hornschuch (1972, p. 8) determined that 'it [was] necessary for anyone wishing to perform this task to have a knowledge of both languages [that is, Latin and Greek]; in addition he must have extremely good eye-sight, which he needs not so much for smaller letters, but for reading precisely every syllable of every word, and indeed every letter' (see also Hargrave 2019, pp. 19–20). From the outset, therefore, editors were expected to be well read and educated, as well as unfailingly pedantic. Approximately seventy years later, in *Mechanick Exercises or, The doctrine of handy-works. Applied to the art of printing*, the first printer's manual published in English for the English print trade (Hargrave 2019, p. 19), Moxon (1683, pp. 260–261) echoed similar sentiments and supplemented the list: correctors 'should [be] well skilled in Languages', 'very knowing in Derivations and Etymologies of Words, very sagacious in *Pointing*, skilful in the *Compositors* whole Task and Obligation, and endowed with a quick eye to espy the smallest *Fault*' (emphasis in original). Editors were therefore expected to have expertise in not just etymology and spelling, grammar and punctuation (known as 'pointing'), but also in understanding, overseeing and correcting the typeset page – the labour of typesetters (or 'compositors') and printers (Hargrave 2019, pp. 44–45).

Much more recently, Targ (1985, pp. 13–14) avowed the 'unceasing' importance of reading to editors, cultivated 'from the earliest days … of childhood'.[5] The well-known reasoning behind this is that future editors acquire knowledge of, and the aptitude to interrogate, texts' 'language, registers and … subtleties' (Kruger 2007, p. 3) through this lifelong experience. For Upton and Maner (1997, p. 2), editors 'must possess … sound knowledge of grammar and usage, flexibility, good judgement, and an eye for consistency and detail'. While admitting that 'only a handful of editors can truly be called "great"', Harnum's (2001, pp. 182–185), enumeration of 'the great editor' includes salesperson, financial realist, press and author advocate, optimist and joymonger. Butcher et al. (2006, p. 1) similarly perceive that a 'good copy-editor is a rare creature: an intelligent reader and a tactful and sensitive critic; someone who cares enough about perfection of detail to spend time checking small points of consistency in someone else's work but has the good judgement not to waste time or antagonize [sic] the author by making unnecessary changes'; adding to the list, Kruger (2007, p. 5) points to editors' ability to 'immerse oneself wholly in a text, to pay simultaneous attention to different textual aspects and levels'.[6] According to Einsohn (2011a, pp. 1–2), furthermore, the 'teachable novice' should also have attained an 'untiring and sharp eye, the ability to read at different speeds, and a good visual memory', a 'well-tuned ear', a 'solid sense of logic', '[editorial] clairvoyance' and 'computer skills', which are crucial for the twenty-first-century editor or, indeed, any

---

[5] Interestingly, Kruger (2007, p. 2) has found a more recent proponent of this 'traditional' ideology, South African publisher Arthur Atwell, who commented online in 2005 that '[good] editors are not made in editorial training courses. As children, good editors read voraciously, nurtured like great sportspeople from an early age. As a result they understand literary detail, subtlety, and the big picture both intuitively and explicitly, and they are ruthless critics of their own work'. See also Law and Kruger (2008, p. 480).

[6] I would counsel against total immersion, particularly for beginners, as maintaining a critical perspective is vital when appraising and correcting content.

publishing professional (Canty and Watkinson 2012, p. 457). These 'paragons with an excellent array of virtues', as Mackenzie (2011, pp. 1–2) has wryly remarked, additionally require communication, social, managerial and administrative skills and imagination and initiative; 'good' editors need to be team players as well. Further to this is the editor's positive 'invisibility' (Butcher et al. 2006, p. 32; Johanson 2006, p. 49; Poland 2007, p. 103; Greenberg 2015, p. 3) – editors tend to be visible on the page if their editing is carried out ineffectually.

When combined, such attributes could be considered to represent an ideal or even a stereotype, regardless of how the word *good* is judged (the word itself connoting, and therefore compounding, subjective value).[7] After all, editors' reality, as Albers and Flanagan (2019, p. 7) eloquently observe, 'is not about creating a grammatically perfect text, but about creating a text that effectively communicates its information' – a seeing 'beyond the page' – to not just a local or national audience but also potentially an international one; editorial practice also involves negotiating editorial excellence with commercial imperatives, such as adhering to exacting deadlines and budgets. However, from my own experience as a book editor since the late 1990s in the Australian educational publishing industry, contemporary editors are expected to have developed, or have the potential to further develop, the personal and professional attributes enumerated previously to an acceptable level when employed by publishers to perform their daily roles and responsibilities. Editors need to exercise critical judgement in both their approach to content and their decision-making; have awareness of grammar, spelling and punctuation and a meticulous eye for detail and consistency (across not just a title but also the publisher's entire list); understand the nature and execution of

---

[7] In an interview with Greenberg (2015, p. 131), American freelance editor and teacher Constance Hale proffers her judgement: 'What makes a difference between a really good editor and a not-so-good editor is the ability to see the potential of the piece and to articulate it for the writer who is doing his or her best but is often lost in the material. The editor can show the writer the path; the editor can understand the material in a way that the writer doesn't, and articulate that for the writer.'

typography; balance gatekeeping and editorial excellence with present and future commercial obligations (what Greco (1990, p. 15) refers to as a 'knowledge worker'); be an imaginative and flexible thinker, problem-solver and team player; possess mental and physical stamina; embrace the task-oriented reality of editorial practice, not just the romantic ideal of publishing; and be an excellent communicator, diplomat and dedicated spokesperson (in fact, salesperson) for the publishers they represent. For example, Ileene Smith, vice president and executive editor at US trade press FSG, imparted the following when interviewed by Greenberg (2015, p. 49): '[I]t's coming up with the right title. It's figuring out how the jacket should look. It's that really painstaking work on the manuscript itself and it's pushing every aspect of the book in the direction of an ideal'.

The aforementioned final enumeration applies generally to the publishing industry, certainly; such attributes though tend to adapt to, or be remoulded for, the specific publishing industry sector for which editors work: scholarly (monographs and journals), trade (general fiction and non-fiction for adults and children), education (primary, secondary and tertiary), professional (legal, financial and informational technology), information and reference, magazines and so on (Poland 2007, pp. 98–99).

## *Learning: Editing and Publishing Pedagogies*

'Modern publishing education in the West', writes Maxwell (2014, p. 1), 'gelled in the late-20th century, largely as an institutional response to a need for trained employees in a stable industry with a well understood set of competencies and skills'. Publishing and editing courses at universities began to emerge as early as the first decades of the twentieth century. The first, according to Woodings (1990, p. 6), was a diploma programme at New York University in the 1930s; the second, in 1947, appears to have been the six-week Radcliffe Publishing Course in Cambridge, Massachusetts (Geiser 1997, p. 13). A faculty chair for *Buchwesen* (meaning 'essence or substance of the book') was established at Gutenberg University, Mainz, in 1949 (Kerlen 2001, pp. 23–24). In France, the first publishing certificate was

offered in the late 1940s (Laham 1990, p. 20).[8] The first publishing programmes in England were established in 1961: a full-time three-year
diploma at Oxford College of Technology for 'pre-experience students'
and a one-year postgraduate course. The first undergraduate programme
was launched at Oxford Polytechnic in 1983 (Woodings 1990, p. 6). In
Canada, the Banff Publishing Workshop was launched in the early 1980s,
which was modelled on the Radcliffe course, the publishing programme at
Simon Fraser University, in the early 1990s (Maxwell 2014, p. 2). Moving
further afield, annual courses have been running in Tokyo since 1967,
'sponsored by the Asian Cultural Center for UNESCO' and 'supported
by the Japanese Ministry for Education and the Japan Book Publishers'
(Montagnes 1997, p. 246); in Africa, seven postgraduate courses were
established during 1975–1991, with four in Nigeria and one each in
Kenya, South Africa and Zimbabwe (Crabbe 2016, p. 237); and in
Australia, the Royal Melbourne Institute of Technology (now RMIT
University) introduced in 1988 the Graduate Diploma in Editing and
Publishing, and the first graduate programme in the country was founded
in 1989 by Macquarie University in Sydney (Poland 2007, p. 107).[9]

It is necessary to acknowledge here that the scope of editing programmes can differ: specific courses might be designated editing only,
focusing principally on copy-editing and structural editing, while others
might be dedicated to the wider editorial components and responsibilities in
the publishing process, such as project management of (internal and external) stakeholders and undertaking internships. The methods of teaching and
assessment necessarily adjust according to these approaches and foci; this is
demonstrated later by comparing Greco's (1990) publishing-oriented marking approach, for example, with Masse's (1985) editing-focused theoretical–
practical synergy.

---

[8]  Lanham (1990, p. 20) notes that Cercle de la Librairie offered a 'professional'
    course in 1908; however, this was 'directed, at first, toward bookselling' as '[no]
    one thought at the time that publishing courses were necessary, but publishers
    needed an effective sales force'.
[9]  Swinburne Institute of Technology, in Melbourne, provided a unit on editing in
    the early 1980s (Poland 2007, p. 107).

Research on editing and publishing pedagogies to date has witnessed two broad perspectives: a structural market-oriented approach and a theoretical–practical union, or synergy. Notable examples of these are examined later. This review intends to not just present a historical appraisal but also illuminate how pedagogies have evolved. Such an appraisal, however, especially for the twenty-first century, comes with a caveat and collegial empathy owing to the pedagogical challenges posed by persistent technological change and disruption; this was aptly communicated by Maxwell (2014, p. 2):

> Today, in the century's second decade, the world of publishing is [sic] changed. The very idea of a stable industry with stable labour requirements is in some question. More to the point, the idea of a stable *curriculum*, or at least a stable set of core competencies for publishing graduates and would-be employees, is also in question. Today, markets are disrupted; distribution and sales channels are in flux; production is a quagmire of emerging and yet unstable technologies. Even editorial curriculum, which perhaps has the best claim to an idealist vision of what it aims to do, has been disrupted, especially in periodical publishing. In light of all this, what is a university to teach, exactly? How can anyone craft meaningful curriculum in such circumstances? (emphasis in original)

Nevertheless, as demonstrated by Greco (1990), the publishing industry has needed to respond to persistent technological change and disruption since the late 1980s with the emergence of, for example, desktop publishing, which necessitated the frequent updating of knowledge and skills by educators and industry practitioners alike. That is, publishing continues to be a dynamic, ever-changing industry relentlessly faced with complex challenges; those that educators and practitioners need to address in the 2020s are no less integral than those from the late 1980s – though today both have the benefit of hindsight.

## Structural Market-Oriented Pedagogy

The approach of Greco (1990), one of the earliest authors to have studied publishing pedagogy, could be perceived as being primarily structural (or, more pertinently, organisational), always mindful of the publishing industry within this context and how this industry is susceptible to frequent, significant change. He observed at the time that the 'cozy, fraternal world of publishing ... sustained a series of events (some unpleasant, most of them necessary, especially in the marketing and financial management areas) that transformed a significant number of specialized [sic] book or business magazine companies into publishing and information-processing corporations, many with global operations' (p. 13). Greco was also conscious of how changes to, and in, industry affected publishing education. In the abstract preceding his article 'Teaching publishing in the United States', Greco expressed his intention to offer both 'theoretical and practical ideas about teaching publishing' (p. 12); however, these ideas relate overall to *how* teaching publishing should be executed within a global context: 'academicians must consider the need to reevaluate [sic] their research projects, courses and seminars, faculty development programs [sic], and their professional ties to the publishing community if their training is to remain meaningful to both students and employers' (pp. 14–15).

To arrive at a theoretical but practical framework to underpin publishing education, specifically at New York University, Greco posed a series of questions:

> What *theoretical* framework might we work within to train the next generation of publishing leaders? What will publishers need to know in order to become and remain effective executives? What problems are inherent in trying to be effective within large, global publishing and information processing corporations? (p. 15; emphasis in original)

Greco's repetition of the word *effective* when asking these questions is deliberate: the framework that he developed was influenced by Drucker's *Management: Tasks, Responsibilities, and Practices* (1974); according to Greco (1990, p. 15), Drucker 'maintained that *the* key area of managerial concern was, and always will be, "effectiveness"' (emphasis in original). That is, how can the publishing industry's 'knowledge workers' – namely authors and editors – be managed to perform their creative work appropriately? The reason for this is such work, which has the potential to be 'unpredictable' but has substantial implications for a company's 'performance and financial results', cannot be supervised in a manner traditionally expected within, or by, industry; an effective manager is one who understands the nature of creative work and assists knowledge workers in the execution of this work. The movement of Greco's framework from theoretical to practical occurs when educating 'the next generation of publishing leaders', who eventually become the overseers of knowledge workers in the publishing industry. In this way, Greco's publishing pedagogy was market-oriented and 'composed of courses and seminars that deal with *specific* problems and areas of concern to publishers (for example global publishing, mergers and acquisitions, scholarly publishing, or trends in the book industry)' (p. 16; emphasis in original).

Consequently, the postgraduate publishing programme at New York University was structured with a market-centred mindset, targeting primarily students who had completed undergraduate studies in the liberal arts, humanities and sciences. This involved forming an advisory board of industry leaders 'to give timely, practical advice to university-based academicians' (p. 16), developing an interdisciplinary publishing curriculum, providing students with practical experience of the publishing industry through internships, employing and maintaining a teaching and research faculty ('you cannot develop a first-rate educational program [sic] based on the work on adjuncts' (p. 17)), building and maintaining relationships with professional publishing associations, and undertaking research on the publishing industry to respond to 'the lack of attention paid within the academic community to the world of publishing' (p. 18).[10]

---

[10] Johnson and Royle (2000, p. 19) similarly urged industry and universities in Britain to respond in unison to the following challenges: 'the implications of technological change, the need to enhance the provision of and support for continuing professional development, the reassessment of the industry's approach to its international market, the basis for collaboration between industry and the academic community, the maintenance of professional standards [and] the underpinning research agenda'.

Baensch (2004, p. 32) proffered a similar structural market-oriented approach to Greco (1990): 'There are two different factors for professional education: one is *skill*-specific and other is *management* specific' (emphasis in original). Such education is administered with the knowledge that the publishing industry had been undergoing transition, affected by '[in] the last fifteen years four major trends': digital technology, globalisation (mergers and acquisitions), concentration of the market at the same time being infiltrated by new online entrepreneurs and more titles being published for fewer readers in new media-saturated markets (p. 30). The skills-specific component of this education therefore needed to account for these trends and educate students about how they influenced the work of myriad stakeholders in the publishing industry. For example, the editorial skills of commissioning editors in the magazine or journal publishing sectors are distinct from those editors developing content for online spaces; editorial skills generally differed from the skills required by designers, production, marketing and sales, finance and distribution to support the creative endeavour of editors and other knowledge workers. This interdepartmental mindset naturally points to, and connects with, the next set of skills to be cultivated as part of students' university education – that of management:

> We must also think about education of the *management* of the publishing process. It is one thing to learn the skill; it is another thing to manage the interrelationships of the skills. And we cannot as a publishing industry leave it to the 6 or 7 global conglomerates. The global conglomerate can train from within because it has the human resources. The global conglomerates are not only purchasing companies, they also purchase inventory, purchase imprints, and the 'global conglomerate' is also purchasing skilled staff and management. The value of experienced and trained human resources are part of the equation. (Baensch 2004, p. 32; emphasis in original)

Reminiscent again of Greco (1990), Baensch (2004) questioned how such publishing education was to be effectively achieved, especially for national, regional and international contexts. Baensch signposted seven challenges that educators needed to consider when developing curriculum; for example, '[supporting] cultural diversity by being responsive to the unique needs of the publishing industries', considering the rapidly changing technologies and how these impact on industry and publishing education by concentrating on 'such areas as electronic publishing, copyright and licensing in the electronic environment, [and] international management and marketing' and '[establishing] standards for the levels, content and quality of the education and training programs [sic] on a worldwide basis'. These challenges were presented without definite resolutions, though Baensch welcomed input from interested parties to assist with 'training the next generation of publishers in all parts of the world' (p. 33).[11]

## Theoretical–Practical Synergy

Similarly to Greco (1990), Masse (1985) was an early contributor to discourse on editing and publishing pedagogies, though employing an explicitly theoretical–practical method, or synergy, for his graduate students of an Advanced Workshop in Technical and Professional Communication at New Mexico State University. His guiding philosophy was that students developed their own theories of editing through technical research, instruction and practice. He observed that 'courses can be structured to help students examine research on editing, practice [sic] editing, and develop their own theories of editing' (p. 34). Masse connected theory

---

[11]  The importance of a market-oriented skills–management approach was signposted earlier by Johnson and Royle (2000, p. 13): 'Overall, employers suggested that their problems in recruiting and training staff pointed to four priorities for development: management skills, Information Technology, desk editing, and page mark-up skills. Interestingly, many of the attributes which they most value are not part of the vocational curriculum in higher education: co-operation, willingness to learn, written communications skills, dependability/reliability, self-motivation, consideration, teamwork, flexibility, commitment and planning ability.'

and practice by requiring students to complete two broad-based activities. The first entailed students '[d]eveloping and using levels of edit and editorial dialogue in editing workshops'; these levels of edit, from simple to more complex, were derived from two essays by Buehler published in 1977 and 1981:[12]

> Buehler's essays provide us with an organized [sic] approach to editing through the concept of 'levels of edit'. The concept, which Buehler developed for editing at the Jet Propulsion Laboratory (JPL), involves defining types of editing and then combining them into different levels according to the amount of editing needed in a manuscript. The types of editing activity include coordination, policy, integrity, screening, copy clarification, format, mechanical style, language, and substantive. (p. 34)

Masse adapted Buehler's levels of edit to structure the unit and thereby provide students with an approach that could be applied to 'almost any editing situation' (p. 35). In these workshops, more particularly, students worked in groups to appraise select manuscripts according to Buehler's levels of edit and to determine which aspects of the manuscripts required more attention than others. The editorial dialogue for this first activity pertained to instructing students on techniques that editors use to talk '*with*, not *at*, writers', namely, receptive listening, a guide for analysis (where 'the editor uses a guide ... to check what has been done and the writer uses a guide to see what needs work'), notetaking and empathetic role mirroring (p. 36).

The second of Masse's activities involved students '[d]eveloping theories of editing process through research and experience' (p. 34; see also Flanagan (2019, p. 29)). To devise their individual theories, students wrote a research

---

[12]  M. F. Buehler 1977, 'Controlled Flexibility on Technical Editing: The Levels-of-Edit Concept at JPL' in *Technical Communication*, First Quarter, 24: pp. 1–4; and 'Defining the Terms in Technical Editing: The Levels of Edit as a Model', *Technical Communication*, Fourth Quarter, 28: pp. 10–15.

essay by critiquing and synthesising secondary sources from a literature search and then explaining their resulting theory of the editing process. Masse observed that students often utilised their own professional experience to describe their editorial theories. Through both activities, Masse endeavoured to not just teach students requisite editing skills but also provide them with an understanding of the scope and the techniques to respond to future editing challenges.

Chaffanjon (1994, p. 38) likewise recommended almost a decade later a theory–practice approach: 'All theoretical education develops from knowledge and skills that prepare students to practice [sic] their profession'; this approach was further coupled with close awareness of, and association with, industry. Chaffanjon though was mindful that the scope of industry collaboration was influenced by the state of the market (in his case, France) – that is, 'available employment and possible career paths' (p. 36) and the type of university department that offered the instruction – he posits three relevant fields: the liberal arts and sciences, communication and economics; and the necessity to provide students with a 'broad view of the professions': he observed that 'young people must be exposed to the whole industry if they are to have the opportunity to develop a career' (p. 37). To equip students with this whole-industry picture, Chaffanjon determined that publishing education be founded on a pedagogic progression that united theory and practice – more specifically, 'theoretical reflection and practical training'. For the successful provision of the latter, industry collaboration was vital. The triumvirate of theory, practice and industry culminated in knowledge 'transform[ing] into real abilities' (p. 38).

Adapted from Gile's (1995) *Basic Concepts and Models for Interpreter and Translator Training*,[13] the process-oriented approach has been advocated by Kruger (2007), of North-West University, South Africa. Kruger's (2007, p. 9) approach, which prioritises process over product, embodies a response to the perceived shortcomings of 'most approaches to the training of editors': the 'micro' or minutial editing (spelling, grammar and sentence

---

[13] Daniel Giles 1995, *Basic Concepts and Models for Interpreter and Translator Training*. Amsterdam: John Benjamins.

construction) and 'macro' or substantive editing (structure, consistency and clarity) of content; both the 'ideological functions of texts within a particular society' and the 'role of the editor in an ideological contested context'; typography and layout; hard-copy and on-screen editing; and the professional components of all such work: 'ethics, interpersonal aspects, professional behaviour, professional bodies, and the importance of professionalisation'. The reasons for these shortcomings include educators' lack of close supervision of students in comparison to the mentoring and shadowing of graduates that tend to occur in-house in industry,[14] the 'artificial' nature of the texts that students are exposed to because they are generally not representative of real-world contexts, and often university educators' dearth of industry experience, making such educators incognisant of the commercial realities of publishing (p. 3). According to Kruger, the process-oriented approach is highly practical, albeit with a 'sufficient' theoretical foundation, and benefits students by apprising them of the 'often (covert) decision-making' that occurs during the editing process (p. 2). That is, Kruger emphasises to her students that editing involves a 'series of decisions or choices' (p. 11) that need to be made about texts; through this consideration, a sequential model of editing emerges in which problems that arise in the editing process can be categorised and resolved:

> Learners do a variety of editing assignments, involving different text types, different categories of problems, and different levels of integration of categories of problems. Assignments usually follow a clear delineation of the aspects learners are expected to master, as well as relevant reading and class discussions.
>
> [. . .] Learners are required to annotate all problematic editing decisions, thus forcing them to motivate their choices and reflect on their decision-making process during the editing process. Sometimes we use unmarked (draft) assignments as the starting point for discussions during which learners

---

[14] Many would understandably argue that educators are endemically time-poor and without sufficient resources to conduct this level of supervision.

compare and motivate their choices, after which they do a revised assignment for assessment. More often, however, we use marked assignments in class discussions to facilitate discussion on various editing approaches and decision-making processes. (pp. 11–12)

Dunbar (2017, p. 307), however, extends Kruger's (2007) artificiality to students' assessments: 'Ultimately . . ., the artificiality of assignments in which errors have been deliberately embedded makes me uncomfortable. I worry that a consciously introduced variety of mistakes underprepares students to deal with the subtle and complicated error patterns that tend to appear over the course of lengthier manuscripts'. Dunbar also observes that this artificiality precludes the collaborative, often organic work that resides in a publishing house.

## *Doing: An Editorial Performance*

### Learning-by-Doing (and University Presses)

Greenberg (2018), University of Roehampton (England), and O'Shaughnessy et al. (2019), RMIT University (Melbourne, Australia), also apply theory–practice pedagogy, albeit their practice-based, or 'doing', component is envisaged entirely differently for twenty-first-century students. They have identified that experiential learning theory (ELT) underpins their publishing and editing pedagogies; this theory was developed by Kolb in his *Experiential Learning: Experience as the Source of Learning and Development* (1984). Learning is defined according to ELT as 'the process whereby knowledge is created through the transformation of experience' (Kolb and Kolb 2005, p. 194, 2009, p. 44), as similarly intimated by Chaffanjon (1994) earlier. It is a ubiquitous learning process. For Greenberg (2018, pp. 176–177), publishing education is 'theory in action':

When brought to the academy, the principles of experiential knowledge are often articulated using the language of 'reflective practice'. This draws on the concept of the

experiential learning cycle, a model of learning-by-doing
whereby concrete experience is followed by reflective observation, theory-building and then further experimentation.

The framework in which theory in action is applied is, what is termed, 'the
apprentice model of the art studio' (p. 177), where students are offered
opportunities in safe environments to trial and interrogate decisions made
during the editing process.

The apprenticeship model is also utilised by O'Shaughnessy et al. (2019,
p. 30), where skills are acquired 'via on-the-job learning in publishing' –
this on-the-job learning or learning-by-doing occurs, for example, at RMIT
University where O'Shaughnessy is employed: students completing
a master of writing and publishing are apprenticed to the university teaching
press – the Bowen Street Press – which was established in 2016. For
O'Shaughnessy, it is 'learning-by-interning' (p. 43):

> It is a compulsory subject: an inclusive internship program
> [sic]. This vertically aligned 'studio' is supported by comple-
> mentary technical and theoretical subjects (echoing the way
> entry-level publishing employees learn the broader cultural
> context of their business from meetings and conversations –
> which they may participate in or simply be witness to). (p. 33)

O'Shaughnessy explains that at the Bowen Street Press, not only are
students exposed to diverse genres, such as fiction, non-fiction, journals,
poetry and digital publishing, but also they experience myriad publishing
roles at different stages of production to create publications in various
formats – colour, black and white, and marketing and website material.
Moreover, students are mentored by industry practitioners during this time.
Through this, students have the opportunity to acquire both technical and
interpersonal skills: 'For every hard skill – such as copy-editing, proofreading, laying out pages or seeking copyright permissions – there is an
equally important soft skill that future producers need to master: from basic
professional communication to diplomacy, persuasiveness, resourcefulness
and time management' (p. 44).

The specific ELT theory that guides the pedagogy of Bowen Street Press is Kolb's cycle of experiential learning; O'Shaughnessy explains the application of Kolb's cycle with reference to industry: 'Learning that progresses in line with Kolb's cycle (from concrete experience to reflective observation to abstract conceptualization to active experimentation) both reflects the way our industry works – as producers move from project to project – and is well suited to the current challenging publishing context' (pp. 44–45).

## Learning-by-Interning (in Industry)

Modern internships have been defined as 'supervised introductory career opportunities provided in partnership between academic institutions and professional organizations [sic]' (Sides and Mrvica 2017, p. 1; Schultz 2019, p. 5). These internships are arranged by coordinators at universities, and interns typically undertake supervised, unpaid work at an organisation for an agreed number of hours each week over a semester. The purpose therefore is to provide students with real-world, practical experience to reinforce the skills acquired at university and/or develop others, as well as offer the potential to network, build relationships and create prospective employment opportunities once they graduate. In Australia, internship placements are offered by, for example, Hardie Grant Media (Siebert n.d.), Internships Downunder,[15] Busybird Publishing,[16] Hachette Australia[17] and the Lifted Brow.[18]

Evidence shows that internships have increased significantly in the twenty-first century, particularly since the global financial crisis that started in 2007 (Durack 2013, p. 249). For example, Shade and Jacobsen

---

[15] Internships Downunder, 'Publishing Internship', www .internshipsdownunder.com/internship/publishing-internship/ (accessed 11 January 2020).

[16] Busybird, 'Internships', www.busybird.com.au/about/internships/ (accessed 11 January 2020).

[17] Hachette Australia, 'Careers', www.hachette.com.au/careers/ (accessed 11 January 2020).

[18] The Lifted Brow, 'Work with Us', www.theliftedbrow.com/work-with-us (accessed 11 January 2020).

(2015, p. 189) observed 'an exponential increase in internships in the United States from 17 per cent of graduation students in 1992 to over 50 per cent in 2008'; Canada has witnessed a similar trend. The rise in internship opportunities coincided with the publishing industry's increased outsourcing of labour to freelance staff (such as editors) and offshore typesetters to limit costs – a preference that emerged in the 1970s and 1980s with the rise of multinational conglomerates (Poland 2007; Bridges 2017). The popular trend to accept interns in industry has garnered criticism and concern for industry's ethical practice, which dictates that interns should not replace paid in-house employees. Florence (2013, p. 17) has observed the trend within the Australian publishing industry to profit from unpaid internships: 'In a report from the Fair Work Ombudsman (FWO) earlier [in 2013], internships were found to be increasing in areas where there was high demand but few positions, including media, marketing, and PR, with evidence that "a growing number of businesses are choosing to engage unpaid interns to perform work that might otherwise be done by paid employees"'.

Nevertheless, internships – or learning-by-interning – have the potential to provide valuable hands-on experience, as well as future employment opportunities, as articulated by a former publishing student of mine at The University of Melbourne, Abigail Cini (2018):

> An internship is a process of self-discovery and exploration. There are many roles in publishing – editorial, cover design, permissions, marketing, royalties. It is a chance to try out different roles and see what suits you best. You might even enjoy a role of which you thought; *No way! I wouldn't like that!*
>
> I have learned so much as an intern at Ford Street Publishing. The knowledge I have gained about book production and the publishing industry is invaluable. On a personal level, it has reaffirmed my passion for working in this industry and with authors. My advice is to be open to any experience, paid or unpaid, that will strengthen your skills and confidence.

An important observation emerging from the previously mentioned appraisal of publishing and editing pedagogies is that none of the scholars use the term *transition* when considering graduates' movement from academia to industry; the one approximating this is Chaffanjon (1994, p. 38), who used *transform* to articulate how the theory–practice–industry triumvirate empowers knowledge to become ability. Universities' purview should never be reduced to skills acquisition for students; however, publishing and editing pedagogies form part of students' 'professional education' (Maxwell 2014, p. 6), one that needs to recognise and address the realities of the publishing market in the short to medium term – such as fewer in-house positions advertised, limited resources in-house to provide mentoring for junior staff and industry's skill-intensive work conducted in complex, digital environments – as this is the market that their graduates will be thrust into. The concept of *transition* therefore needs to be applied to pedagogy from students' first year of study and maintained in the foreground until their graduation.

## Transition Pedagogy

Transition pedagogy was developed by Kift and Nelson (2005) to provide academic institutions with 'a framework for the development of an effective and supportive first year university experience' (O'Donnell et al. 2015, p. 75). The reasoning behind this, according to Kift (2015, p. 52), is that 'whatever an individual's prior experiences, making a successful transition to university is never a given. While many students adjust relatively easily, thrive and survive – many do not and consider leaving'. Therefore, transition pedagogy assists in creating a unifying structure in which students feel belonging and engage with university culture and learning in a sequential, self-evaluative way and, through this, ensuring student retention to a higher probability as these experiences nurture students' sense of purpose and understanding of the relevance of their knowledge and skills building now and into the future.

Subsequent research has applied transition pedagogy to not just capstone years (McNamara et al. 2015; Butler et al. 2017) but also the whole-of-university experience for undergraduate students (O'Donnell 2015; O'Donnell et al. 2015). For the latter, transition pedagogy therefore embodies a 'curriculum-integrated approach that enables a smooth, supported shift into and through higher education and a successful transition from the university to the world of work and lifelong learning' (O'Donnell et al. 2015, p. 73). Bunney (2017, p. A23) has reported that students confront similar challenges and exhibit similar needs when transitioning to postgraduate study; however, her research has revealed that the nature of graduate students' difficulties had not been recognised at an institutional level. The focus here for this book is therefore principally on postgraduate students (as they most often enrol in editing and publishing programmes) embracing university culture and learning – both understanding the purpose of their study and its relevance – from their first year of study to transitioning to industry.

## *Methodology*

A mixed-methods approach of two online surveys, three semi-structured interviews and ethnographic practice was applied to obtain quantitative and qualitative information (see the appendices for the survey and interview questions). One survey of twenty-five questions was designed for educators in editing and publishing programmes, and another of twenty questions for their graduates. Owing to this book's size, containing the scope was vital: rather than undertaking randomised distribution, which could result in data becoming unmanageable, specific educators at well-established programmes were approached to circulate the online survey links among department staff to complete anonymously. Fourteen responses from educators were received between December 2019 and February 2020. Educators also kindly forwarded the online student survey link to their graduates to complete anonymously; the student survey link was additionally publicised via alumni Facebook and Twitter sites. Thirty-seven graduate responses were received in the three-month period.

As stated previously in the introduction, the objective of this book is to take an international perspective, as much as practicable for a book of this size, to understand the state of the discipline – its pedagogy and practical instruction. Therefore, programmes and their graduates in the following countries were approached: Australia, Canada, England, Germany, India,

New Zealand, Scotland, South Africa and the United States of America. The number of responses to the online surveys was not standardised, however, for each of the 'countries' during the allocated three-month period. For example, for the educator survey, four of the fourteen respondents were from England, three were from Australia, two from New Zealand, one from Canada, one from Scotland, one from South Africa, one from the United States and one from Germany. Also, the typically non-teaching period between December 2019 and February 2020 was judged at the start of the project to be more ideal for educators than during the semester. The initial judgement about the December–February period proved mistaken to an extent: it made contacting educators and graduates a little more difficult, even with the digital affordances of social media and educators personally distributing the survey link to their graduates. Hence, future research for a larger project would extend the response time to obtain more standardised results.

Closed and open questions were included in the online surveys. For educators, questions were related to whether they had been previously employed, or continue to be employed, in the publishing industry; their programmes' specific structures and objectives; (digital) editorial pedagogy applied across the programme; their programmes' research strengths; student enrolments and results; whether their programmes' operate a teaching press; and if so, how these teaching presses operated. For graduates, questions addressed their experiences of the editing and publishing programmes; their programmes' relevance to the workplace; the critical and industry skills they believe they acquired at the university that translated to industry and those skills only obtained on the job; and opinions relating to programme improvement, if necessary.

For the semi-structured interviews, questions were related to the types of programmes from which employees graduated; whether these employees upon employment possessed the skills and/or confidence to complete their roles' daily responsibilities and to an acceptable standard; whether the publishing companies provided in-house training, or were employees required to obtain additional training elsewhere; whether the interviewees had relationships with academia in terms of providing guest lectures, accepting internships and/or acting as consultants; and whether they had assisted with, or provided advice for, developing, designing and/or revising university courses.

Three semi-structured interviews with an editor at Melbourne University Publishing (academic and scholarly monographs), two managing editors at Cambridge University Press, Australia (academic and professional and education), and a publisher/managing editor at Omnibus Books, an imprint at Scholastic Australia (trade and children's publishing), took place between January and February 2020, either face to face in Melbourne, Australia, or via conference calls. All interviews were recorded, and material appearing in this book was approved by interviewees. While interviewing only Australian publishers does not conform to the international perspective taken for this book, it serves various important purposes: first, scant research has been undertaken for the Australian context; second, the three-month fieldwork period allocated for this project necessitated using my own local contacts to organise the interviews as effectively as possible; and third, the emerging COVID-19 pandemic required organising and conducting the interviews quickly. Hence, similar to the limitation identified regarding the online surveys, future research would involve widening the scope to international publishing stakeholders. Nonetheless, these stakeholders' observations serve to address the majority of the publishing industry: academic, education and trade.

For ethnographic practice, I have been a practising editor of print and digital content since the late 1990s, working principally in the Australian educational publishing industry. Additionally, I have taught writing, editing and publishing since submitting my doctorate in 2016 at three Melbourne higher-education institutions. Therefore, I examine this issue from both perspectives – as a practitioner and an educator. My substantial practical experience and insight serve to enrich and support the data obtained from literature reviews, online surveys and interviews; my experience as an educator supports my observations regarding the need to implement transition pedagogy for university programmes.

## Content and Organisation

The structure of this book has been determined predominantly according to the mixed-methods approach applied. Chapter 2, 'Educator Perspectives', analyses data resulting from the online educator survey, with particular attention given to educator demographics, the structuring of editing and publishing programmes, administration and development of pedagogies and the operation of university teaching presses. Chapter 3, 'Graduate Perspectives', conducts identical work for the online graduate survey, focusing on graduate demographics, current employment of graduates and how students have transitioned from university to industry. Chapter 4, 'Industry Perspectives', provides three case studies derived from semi-structured interviews: Melbourne University Publishing; Cambridge University Press, Australia; and Omnibus Books/Scholastic Australia. Key issues addressed in these case studies are internships, industry perceptions of university postgraduate programmes, professional accreditation and how this potentially affects graduates, expectations and background knowledge of graduates when entering industry, suggestions for improvement to university programmes and graduates discerning editorial boundaries in industry – that is, where certain tasks commence and end. Chapter 5, 'Conclusion', draws out the ways in which the previously mentioned findings support a 'transition' approach that serves to form a holistic practice-led pedagogy (*being*, *learning* and *doing*) for students of editing and publishing programmes.

## 2 Educator Perspectives

### Being *and* Doing*: Demographics*

Fourteen educators working in editing and publishing programmes anonymously completed an online survey of twenty-five closed and open questions between December 2019 and February 2020; no personal information was requested. The countries in which these educators resided, and therefore taught, were England (4 respondents, or 28.57%), Australia (3 respondents, or 21.43%), New Zealand (2 respondents, or 14.29%), Canada (1 respondent, or 7.14%), Scotland (1 respondent, or 7.14%), South Africa (1 respondent, or 7.14%), the United States (1 respondent, or 7.14%) and Germany (1 respondent, or 7.14%). Regrettably, none of the educators approached in India completed the online survey. The most common positions held by these educators were associate professor and lecturer (each with 3 respondents, or 21.43%); next were professor, senior lecturer and assistant professor (each with 2 respondents, or 14.29%); and the least common were senior tutor and tutor (each with 1 respondent, or 7.14%). Most educators were employed on a full-time (8 respondents, or 57.14%) or part-time (4 respondents, or 28.57%) basis; though one educator worked on a full-time contract, and another as a casual (or 7.14% each).

Most educators (12 respondents, or 85.71%) indicated that they had industry experience, either prior to being employed in academia or ongoing. In terms of the duration of experience, one-third of educators had 1–5 years of experience, and one-quarter had 6–10 years; there were significantly fewer for 11 or more years (see Figure 1). The twelve educators specified experience for the following publishing sectors: trade (4 respondents, or 33.33%), education (3 respondents, or 25%) and academic (3 respondents, or 25%). Of these, one educator identified that their experience comprised both education and academic publishing; a second, a mixture of trade and academic (namely, museum publishing); and a third, a mixture of trade and magazines. Furthermore, a fourth commented that they had 'previously worked in scholarly publishing; [and] currently work in trade and self-publishing alongside teaching work'.

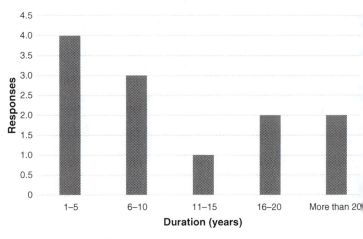

Figure 1 Duration of industry experience of educators

The most common type of work performed in industry by educators was editorial (5 respondents, or 41.67%), commissioning/publishing (3 respondents, or 25%), with production (1, or 8.33%) and marketing (1 respondent, or 8.33%) least. However, qualitative feedback pointed to experience across different positions and/or departments: one educator commented that they had worked for 'a small organisation so I did editorial, commissioning/ publishing and production'; a second, editorial and commissioning; a third was also involved in design; and a fourth, digital production and workflow management. A fifth worked as a consultant.

In terms of the current research strengths or interests, educators' predominant expertise ranges from historical (8 responses, or 57.14%) to contemporary print culture (10 responses, or 71.43%), which includes more specifically digital publishing (10 responses, or 71.43%), trade publishing (8 responses, or 57.14%) and design and production (6 responses, or 42.86%). The least predominant strengths or interests comprised academic publishing (3 responses, or 21.14%) and educational publishing and publishing and editing pedagogy (each with 2 responses, or 14.29%). One other

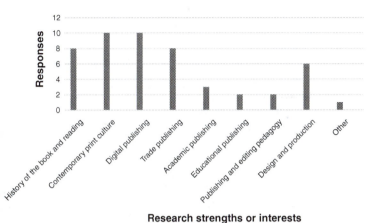

**Research strengths or interests**

Figure 2 Research strengths or interests of educators

educator indicated that their research strength or interest was authorship (see Figure 2). The lack of expertise or interest in academia for educational publishing is noteworthy and has been observed elsewhere (Canty and Watkinson 2012, p. 460; Albers and Flanagan 2019, p. 9). This is also evidenced by student feedback about course limitations for this publishing sector and the importance of educational publishing to the publishing market overall. For example, the Australian publishing industry earned $1.954 billion in 2018. Of this, sales of educational print products amounted to $577 million and for digital, $194 million, which represented approximately 40 per cent of all sales (PWC 2018).

## Learning: *Structuring Editing and Publishing Programmes*
The university courses available for editing and publishing students, viewed substantively, were diverse: ranging from undergraduate to postgraduate coursework and higher research degrees. Educators were requested to select from a multiple-choice list of courses, from which they could choose more than one option. The most common courses offered were doctorates

(PhDs), with 9 responses (or 64.29%); master of arts coursework with minor thesis, with 8 responses (or 57.14%); and bachelor of arts and graduate diploma, each with 5 responses (or 35.71%; see Figure 3). One educator specified that their publishing-specific course was a master of publishing degree; furthermore, this educator explained that 'a number of students [are] pursuing PhDs in "Publishing" who are currently enrolled via the "individualized [sic] interdisciplinary studies" program [sic] as we do not have a PhD program of our own'.

Student numbers were typically more for undergraduate courses than postgraduate and higher research. For example, one educator from Germany explained that '[we] have about 600 students in Book Studies in Mainz 420 BA course of study [and] 180 MA course of study approx. 1 dozen PhD students'; and another enumerated the following: 'Undergraduate – 30–40 students a year Postgraduate – 15 Honours students; 3 master's students; 3 PhD students per year'. However, many editing and publishing courses were offered as master's and higher research only: 'Taught Postgraduates: ~50 [all are enrolled in the MLitt but some will exit with

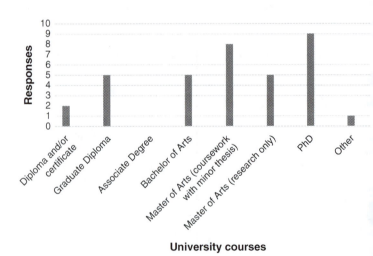

**University courses**

Figure 3 University courses available for editing and publishing students

graduate certificates if they fail to complete their dissertations] PhD students: ~8'. Such courses also tended to be delivered as smaller classes: for one educator, 'The Graduate Diploma in Publishing (Applied) is a one-year full-time course with a maximum class size of 20'; and for another, 'Young students straight our [sic] of their bachelor degrees, mostly, with the odd student with some work experience (though not necessarily in publishing)'. An additional educator pointed to editing and publishing being offered as undergraduate minors only: 'We run a cohort based Masters for 18 students. We have three PhD students We offer an Undergraduate Minor in Print and Digital Publishing that serves upwards of 200 students whose majors are in Communications, English, Business, and Design'.

To gauge the more specific nature of editing and publishing programmes, educators were requested to select from a multiple-choice list of subjects; they could choose more than one option (see Figure 4). The most common subjects offered by universities included 'contemporary publishing industry' (14 respondents, or 100%), 'the business of publishing' (13 respondents, or 92.86%), 'print production and design' (12 respondents, or 85.71%), 'copy-editing and proofreading' (11

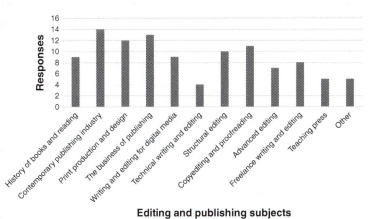

**Editing and publishing subjects**

Figure 4 Editing and publishing subjects offered at universities

respondents, or 78.57%) and 'structural editing' (10 respondents, or 71.43%). The least common were 'teaching press' (5 respondents, or 35.71%) and 'technical writing and editing' (4 respondents, or 28.57%). The response here for offering a teaching press subject could be perceived as somewhat misleading as 7 respondents (50%) indicated later in the survey that their programmes operated a teaching press; for technical writing and editing, the result is expected given student feedback on the lack of specificity in university programmes. Other subjects offered at universities comprised the history of publishing, history of libraries, book cultures/the book as object, marketing, publicity, professional practice, project management ('running a team to publishing a book') and typesetting. Furthermore, one respondent explained they 'also have three courses in digital publishing and digital media from a strategic/theoretical/practical perspective, but aren't writing/editing focused'.

## Administration and Development of Pedagogies

Educators were requested to describe the editing and publishing pedagogies that underpin their programmes, including reference to the design and administration of assessments; an additional question asked educators to contemplate how traditional pedagogy has changed or been adopted owing to the ongoing digital disruption in the publishing industry. Overall, educators constructed their programmes with theory and practice in mind, albeit expressed at times as distinct components. Most courses were taught and administered both on campus and online (these surveys were completed before the first Melbourne COVID-19 lockdown in late March 2020), focusing on practice-based group work and students completing a combination of traditional, digital-first and online assessments. Educator feedback demonstrating more noticeable separation of theory and practice is provided as follows:

> Publishing history is one disciplinary approach New Media studies and digital convergence another disciplinary approach. This is done by supervisory tuition.

We focus on teaching a combination of skills and theory. The focus has shifted over time from skills on paper, to the use of digital tools and software, but the theory hasn't really changed. Students are taught using face-to-face lectures, practical sessions in computer labs, and supplementary materials on our online system. Assessment is also mixed, combining written tests, practical exercises, projects or assignments, and digital tests such as quizzes.

For . . . coursework students (i.e. BA and MA) wishing to study editing and publishing, there are really only two units that offer this specific focus. These two units are hosted within the Professional Writing and Publishing major. There is a unit focused on editing, and there is a unit focused on publishing (which, of course, includes editing, but it also includes marketing, design, etc.). In the editing unit, there are three assessments: a structural editing assessment, a copy-editing assessment, and a proofreading assessment. The copy-editing assessment is the only one that has really responded to digital disruption (though it's hardly a recent manifestation of digital disruption) because it requires students to use Microsoft Word's track changes feature. In the publishing unit, there are three assessments: a query letter assessment, a marketing plan assessment, and a design assessment. In this case, the design assessment is the only one that has really responded to digital disruption (though again it's hardly a recent manifestation of digital disruption) because it requires students to complete their design work using Adobe InDesign.

The third educator's feedback about digital disruption is problematic: disruption cannot be reduced to applying the track changes function in Microsoft Word or completing design work using Adobe InDesign as these have featured in editorial, design and typesetting work for more than two decades. The track changes feature was introduced in Word for Windows in 1995, and Adobe InDesign began supplanting Adobe PageMaker as standard software from the mid-1990s. Furthermore, educators need to avoid complacency as disruption to editors' work continues, particularly in the COVID-19 environment: 'The tools and technology of writing and editing within the corporate environment are changing rapidly and resulting in a change of the editorial role' (Albers and Flanagan 2019, p. 11). This conclusion is not original nor recent, with industry professionals such as Peter Donoughue (2013, p. 15), former Managing Director of John Wiley and Sons Australia, commenting on it for some time: 'We are in the throes of a digital transition that is radically challenging our traditional operations, structures, habits of mind and very identities'.

The most significant disruption that relates to editorial practice specifically, and publishing more generally, is the movement from print to digital occurring from the mid-2010s as noted by the second educator. Editorially, this movement applies not just to editing manuscripts on-screen, typically using Microsoft Word and the track changes function to ensure transparency between the author and editor (though the use of track changes is more a policy issue as part of editorial procedures) but also undertaking proof-correction of typeset pages on-screen using Adobe Acrobat Reader (Hargrave 2014) or, increasingly, InCopy. For the publishing industry more widely, the disruption relates to digital workflows through the entire production cycle, such as using the cloud to upload (and download) authors' manuscripts; deliver these to freelance editors and other contracted staff, if necessary; supply typeset pages as PDF files for correction using Adobe Acrobat Reader and amalgamation from multiple stakeholders (author, editor, proofreader, publisher and indexer, to name a few) into a master set; return these to production and/or typesetters (most often offshore); and transfer final manuscript files (as PDFs) to printers (typically offshore). The decades-long, non-disruptive practices of applying track changes in Microsoft Word and using Adobe InDesign for design and typesetting were observed by one of the educators surveyed, although editing on-screen was standard practice well before 2003, at least for half a decade:

> Disruption is a bit of a myth and hasn't really been an issue for us. The program [sic] has been digitally oriented from its inception (in 2003) with editing for the web taught from the outset and with the assumption that books are non-device

specific. For instance, we have taught editing on screen since 2003, well in advance of it being taken up as standard practice by the industry.

While not agreeing entirely with the view that disruption is 'a myth' given the movement from print to digital and the concomitant impact on digital workflows, this educator's additional observations about the integration of theory and practice are apposite, rather than maintaining a more noticeable separation: 'Highly interactive and very practical with subjects being taught via workshops in computer labs in many cases, and via simulations, case-based learning, etc. in other cases'. This more interactive learning-by-doing – or knowledge building through creation – such as in studios, computer labs and/or practical workshops is reflected in the pedagogies of other educators and, for some, considered to underpin students' 'apprenticeships', albeit with varying success, as expressed by the penultimate respondent below:

> A good deal of our program [sic] is based in collaborative experiential learning, where students design and create things – whether these are editorial artefacts or more material things – and receive multiple rounds of feedback from faculty and industry guests.

> Principles of course after learning through doing. A professional preparation course with a lot of practical assignments and industry involvement.

> Our program is very experiential-learning and project-based focused. For our editorial classes, we work with live manuscripts and real authors, and as students also work within [our teaching] press, all of the editorial work is connected directly with industry.

> We run our course very much as an apprenticeship, so changes in the digital space are constantly being made adn [sic] applied, as our students work directly with publishers.

As a course in Publishing Studies rather than Publishing, we attempt to mix practical assignments with more traditional academic work, although the students often struggle more with the academic work. Students often submit portfolios on digital publishing, editing, and marketing. There is a strong emphasis on group work but also every students [sic] is required to create their own mini-publication over the course of the first two semesters. Recent discussions with colleagues have suggested that the programme has remained largely the same (barring minor tweaks) for the last decade at least and likely much longer, meaning elements of digital publishing are largely sidelined to a dedicated module.

We run our course as an apprenticeship with close connections to local publishing houses and PANZ, the Publishers' Association of New Zealand. Assessments and teaching are updated based on industry requirements and feedback.

The previously mentioned responses reveal educators' recognition of the necessity to involve industry to assist with balancing theory and practice for overall pedagogy. To determine the nature of this involvement, educators were asked to specify with which of the sectors of the publishing industry did their programmes have working relationships in terms of guest lectures, internships and/or advisory consultations; they could select more than one of the options provided. All educators indicated that they had working relationships with stakeholders from trade publishing; 13 (or 92.86%) selected both education and academic publishing; 9 (or 64.29%) for self-publishing; and 8 (or 57.14%) for magazines. Additional relationships listed were those with industry associations: two educators explained that 'We work closely with the Publishers; Association' and 'We also have good connections to the institutions, e.g. reading/literacy organizations, publishers/booksellers association etc.' Another commented that their programme liaised with institutional publishers, such as 'university presses and museum and art gallery presses'. These results point to educators' whole-industry perspective or intention; effective application of this perspective in terms of pedagogy is nevertheless the fundamental concern.

To assess the extent of industry contribution to pedagogy, educators were asked whether they involved, or consulted with, the publishing industry when specific subjects and/or courses were developed, designed and/or revised and, if so, exactly how was industry involved. Most educators (13 respondents, or 92.86%) answered positively to the first question; the remaining educators commented that they 'were not involved in the development of the subjects or coursework'. Of the thirteen educators, one stipulated that industry involvement 'depend[ed] on time'. For the second question, industry contribution related mostly to stakeholders' appointment to advisory boards and the hiring of sessional and/or adjunct staff with industry experience:

> We have an Industry advisory board and regular consultations with publishing professionals before revising our courses.

> Publishers Advisory Board, regular consultation over assignments.

> When I hire sessional tutors for either of the editing and publishing units that we offer, I always hire individuals with a background in the publishing industry. I regularly consult with these individuals about how to revise specific units and/or courses.

> Our advisory board has representatives from govt and trade publishing, and our assessments are moderated by people working in the publishing industry.

> We are very close to the industry and have half a dozen or so industry adjuncts who design and teach subjects in conjunction with in-house staff, plus honorary industry fellows, plus over 40 industry guests per year lecturing in the program [sic], helping out on subject judging panels, etc., and many dozens of internship partners. We stay in contact with them

and with employers of our students (many of whom are former students) and take on board their comments when it comes to keeping our subjects up to date. We are also subject to regular internal formal reviews which involve industry representation.

For other educators, industry involvement appeared more ad hoc and sporadic. One educator explained that industry consultation occurred 'through local SMEs or interview in larger organisations. Sometimes trade shows give opportunities to make contacts'; for a second, questionnaires were distributed 'regularly', and a 'small advisory team' was involved; and for a third, the programme's advisory board was 'currently inactive'. For a fourth, consultation resulted from the programme's own contribution to industry: 'In Germany there is the "Berufsbildungsausschuss" of the publishers and booksellers association, and we are a member'. Lastly, and interestingly, only one educator explicitly referred to their own professional experience in their enumeration: 'Advisory Board, our own professional practice, validation process, industry external examiners'.

### Learning-by-Doing: *Operation of University Teaching Presses*

Half of the fourteen educators' programmes operated a teaching press; for the remainder, three educators cited insufficient funds and/or resources that precluded establishing a teaching press and two indicated that their programmes were in the process of establishing a press. In additional feedback, one educator highlighted collaboration with an adjacent school with a press as a reason for not operating their own ('we don't operate it, the School of art and design do, however we work with them'); and another mentioned that their teaching press was 'more of a laboratory for experimental publishing work, rather than a press that produces a regular list of titles'. Two educators gave precedence to industry partnerships for students' skills acquisition:

> We have strong relationships with local publishers and students are assigned to work on projects with these

publishers during the year, getting real-world experience and connections, in lieu of an in-house press.

We prefer to partner with publishers so that the works our students produce are genuine commercial publications (that have a real market). We always have publishers wanting to partner with us, and they pay a small fee, which contributes to our bottom line. This way of working also allows students to have a greater range of experience with different publishers, authors, mentors and material than if we were running a press.

Content produced from these presses derived from the scholarly output at the programmes' (or other) institutions (4 respondents, or 40%); unpublished authors (3 respondents, or 30%); previously submitted student work (2 respondents, or 20%) and specific calls for papers (1 respondent, or 10%). Educators indicated additional sources in their feedback: for example, 'Orders from within the university and the town', 'Local organisations. Literary contacts' and 'Collaborations with organisations and other departments within the university'.

Teaching presses certainly embody a microcosm of the publishing industry, with students performing specific stakeholder roles to produce, publish and distribute content, both print and digital. The pedagogical objective is that students acquire practical, real-world experience, as evidenced by educator feedback: 'work-based learning. commercial project based'; 'Opportunity for students to engage in live projects with direct contact with authors'; 'To offer students a real-life experience of deadlines and workflow in a commercial publishing house' and 'Giving students the ability to experiment – and fail – in a situation where those risks won't put everyone out of work!'

Of the seven teaching presses, two were entirely student-operated (five educators did not explicitly identify whether their presses were student- or teacher-led):

[Our teaching press] is a completely student-run, award-winning, and nationally distributed publishing company.

> The process of acquiring, marketing, designing and editing any new title is a democratic process that we strive to preserve so that the students are the ones who have a voice in what and how publishing happens.

> Quite simply, students run the press, which is a commercial operation with distribution to the book trade, under staff supervision. Students do all the commissioning, editing, production, marketing, and so on, as part of their assessment in three subjects (one in each semester plus a summer intensive) associated with the press, based on their learnings in other subjects and with input from two staff assigned to teaching press subjects.

The concern here, as signposted previously by an educator, is whether students participating in teaching presses obtain a 'greater range of experience' across publishing sectors. In terms of content, very little diversity manifested in educator feedback – that is, material produced was primarily trade-based in nature – notably literary – intermixed with a little academic publishing: 'Creative Writing, [and] prize anthologies'; 'Memoires, literary fiction, short story collections, historical nonfiction, young adult, speculative fiction, poetry'; 'Commercial non-fiction, academic monographs, historical fiction, literary fiction'; 'Trade books that so far include an Australian colonial fiction series (republications), original literary fiction, and current affairs non-fiction titles' and 'Academic journals and "minigraph" – like shorter occasional works'. One educator pointed to slightly more diversity, though for more ephemeral material, without specifying the exact nature of their titles: 'Its [sic] a digital jobbing press – from posters and banners to books'.

It is understandable that these teaching presses do not publish educational titles, given the development work with teachers and authors relating to a curriculum that typically occurs over months, if not years, before content is written rather than over a semester, which is the usual duration for teaching press units. Nevertheless, student feedback from online surveys has identified a lack of technical instruction in university programmes, which is substantiated by these results. For all educators at universities with teaching presses (i.e. 7 respondents, or 63.64%), however, the success of their graduates in obtaining employment in the publishing industry is attributed to their teaching presses. This potentially points to a disconnect between educators and graduates, which is explored later in this book.

## 3 Graduate Perspectives

### Being *and* Learning: *Demographics*

Thirty-seven graduates of editing and publishing programmes anonymously completed an online survey of twenty closed and open questions between December 2019 and February 2020; no personal information was requested. The age ranges with the highest number of respondents were 26–28 and 40 or older, with 9 for each (24%), and 29–32, with 7 respondents (19%). For the remainder, 1 respondent was aged 18–22 (3%), 3 for 36–39 (8%) and 4 each for 23–25 (11%). In terms of location, 14 respondents resided in the United States (38%), 11 in Australia (30%), 6 in New Zealand (16%), 4 in India (11%) and 2 in England (5%). Interestingly, in a pre-COVID-19 world, countries in which graduates reside sometimes differed from those in which they completed their degrees: the two graduates residing in England graduated from Australian programmes. Meaning there were 13 graduates from Australian universities (or 35%), with 14 from the United States (38%), 6 from New Zealand (16%) and 4 from India (11%).

To gauge their education levels, graduates were asked to identify the undergraduate and/or postgraduate degrees that they had completed. The majority of respondents (36 out of 37) had completed an undergraduate degree or diploma: the most common was bachelor of arts, with English literature, (creative) writing and media and communications majors being most frequently cited; other majors included linguistics, (art) history, journalism and (social) sciences. One respondent completed a diploma in publishing. Of the bachelor of arts graduates, 33 respondents (92%) indicated that their undergraduate degrees had specific relevance to their current positions in the publishing industry. For example, in regard to English literature (the predominant major), 1 respondent explained that, as an editor, 'basic English education was crucial in my development'; a second observed that 'English literature as a major allowed me to be aware of the literary sphere, an invaluable asset in publishing'; and a third stated that their degree was 'relevant in understanding literary references, tropes, style, and writing style in analysis and practice'. Of the three respondents who believed their degree had little to no relevance (8%), one reported that their degree 'was quite broad and had an academic rather than technical focus, so has little relevance to my job'; the second remarked that '[while] my job isn't in publishing per second I use the editing, project management and analytical skills I learned every day'; and the third related that while they had completed a minor in literature as part of this under-graduate degree, '[core] science subjects also can inform aspects of my current role in educational publishing'.

For graduate degrees, respondents most frequently graduated with a master of publishing and communications (or book publishing), with a few obtaining a graduate diploma; other programmes included master of arts in (creative) writing and in English literature. In terms of relevance to their current employment, 32 respondents (94%) indicated there was clear relevance. One respondent explained that '[these] were intense, focussed professional programmes, and I draw on the skills learned daily'; and a second, that 'Yes I work [in] digital educational publishing in a tertiary setting', so 'I utilise many editorial skills I developed in the course'. For one respondent who acquired a marketing role in higher education, not an editorial one:

> I often use the marketing and advertising strategy, planning and execution I developed in marketing courses and experi-ential learning at [the university teaching press]. At my previous jobs in book publishing – as a marketing and metadata specialist and freelance copy editor and proof-reader – I applied the editorial and business of book publish-ing hard skills I learned in the master's program [sic] in addition to soft skills like communication and visioning with a holistic understanding of the book publishing processes and industry trends.

Two respondents obtained their first positions in publishing with com-panies at which they had completed their internships (or work placements). However, of the two respondents (6%) who believed there was little to no relevance, one imparted that their 'degree had relevance to the publishing industry but did not really prepare me for my job in sales'; the other indicated that the nature of this lack of relevance was related to career decision-making, not the course itself: the 'graduate diploma was completed before I decided to switch my career focus to writing and editing, so has little to no relevance to my current position'.

Graduates were next required to select from a list of subjects those that they had completed as part of the publishing programmes at their universities; more than one option could be chosen (see Figure 5). Contemporary publishing industry (35 respondents, or 94.59%), print production and design (35 respondents, or 94.59%), copy-editing and proofreading (35 respondents, or 94.59%), the business of publishing (31 respondents, or 83.78%) and structural editing (31 respondents, or 83.78%) were the most commonly studied. The least included teaching press (16 respondents, or 43.24%) and freelance writing and editing (13 respondents, or 35.14%). Other subjects studied by respondents included project management principles, manuscript assessment, 'technical instruction in tools used – Adobe creative suite etc.', introduction to copyright and intellectual and property law, digital (ebook) design, 'annotation of academic writing' and indexing.

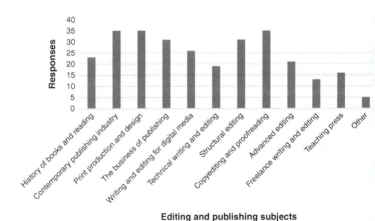

**Editing and publishing subjects**

Figure 5 Subjects studied by graduates

## Students' Doing *Post-Graduation*

### Current Employment of Graduates

Thirty-six respondents indicated that they were employed in the publishing industry, or a publishing-related field, mostly either full time with independent or multinational publishers (see Figure 6). Sixteen respondents (43%) worked in trade, ten respondents (27%) in education and one each (3%) for academic, magazines and self-publishing. Further qualitative responses indicated greater specificity within publishing sectors, such as 'academic and school education (all on remote basis)', 'digital romance publisher', 'museum writer and editor', 'professional services (architecture, engineering, construction)', comics and public library; as well as movement across sectors, such as 'Previously employed in trade nonfiction, currently working in higher education' and 'I am currently an assistant professor of English in a college, but I am also a freelance copy editor who teaches proof-reading, copy-editing, annotation, and indexing in various editing and publishing courses'. Two respondents explained how they conducted their editorial work in non-publishing fields; for example, one imparted the following: 'I work as a content editor in corporate communications for a large regional bank,

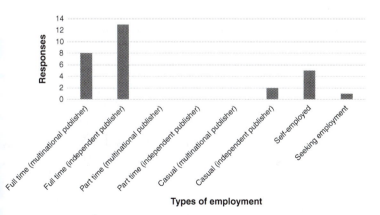

Figure 6 Types of employment obtained by graduates

which draws on my developmental editing, copy-editing, and managing editorial experience from graduate school'.

An adjacent question asked respondents to identify the type of work they currently performed at their workplaces.[19] Seventeen respondents (46%) indicated that they were involved in editorial work; 3 respondents (8%) identified production; 2 respondents (5%) each for design and administration; and 1 respondent (3%) for commissioning/publishing. However, when further qualitative answers were requested, 4 respondents listed sales as their principal work; 3, marketing ('including design and editorial of content marketing' and events management); 2, project management; and 3, a combination of roles ('All of the above except design but I do manage contracted designers/illustrators/videographers etc.' and 'Varied role including editorial, writing, and project management of client contractual publishing').

When asked whether the sector in which they are now employed was where they had initially hoped as students to find employment after completing their tertiary education, 25 respondents (68%) replied positively, while 12 respondents (32%) replied negatively. The reasons for the negative response related to:

- lack of available positions in the industry generally:

> The traditional publishing industry in [New Zealand] had diminished significantly since I graduated.

> Obviously I had hoped to find work in publishing, but the industry is so competitive that I knew the chances were slim. Although corporate communications is not my dream job,

[19] Graduates were asked here to tick one box only, with the knowledge that positions in the publishing industry have become increasingly distinct (using as a guide my own experience working in educational publishing since the late 1990s). Editorial positions often do combine several components/responsibilities, however, such as editing manuscripts and overseeing copyright permissions. For this reason, the 'Other' option was provided for respondents whose positions were multifaceted.

the work is enjoyable and the pay is more than double what I would be making in publishing.

Tried to find freelance or FTE editorial work in actual book publishing or at least actual publications for 6 months after graduating. Still looking after three years at this job.

- lack of available positions in the desired publishing sector:

Not entirely I would love to work in non-fiction trade publishing one day. Educational publishing was an available option to get experience.

I believed I'd be able to get work in a publishing company (assuming either trade or education). I ended up in my current role two years after completing my post-graduate degree and am still not technically 'in' the sector.

As with most graduates I aimed to enter trade fiction, with a particular inclination [sic] for YA publishing, but lack of jobs in the sector at the time of graduation led to a different path.

- indecision about their future while studying:

Was unsure where I was going to end up.

I didn't have a specific sector in mind, but this turns out to be an excellent fit for me.

Whether graduates' present employment fit in with their overall career objective – therefore distinguishing between short- and longer-term career objectives – 30 respondents (81%) answered positively, while 7 respondents (19%) answered negatively. Further qualitative responses by those who answered negatively pointed to reasons identified earlier: lack of overall opportunities in the publishing industry ('I would prefer to be working in more of an Editorial capacity, but there is a lack of such employment in house, and starting freelance with no experience for a CV is near impossible' and 'It wasn't originally – but it has opened up to me that you don't need to work in a publishing company (books, magazines, etc.) to get experience in editing and publishing/publications management'); difficulty obtaining employment in the desired publishing sector ('Still would like to edit books for a living. Not medical reviews' and 'Would like to move to trade publishing one day. Educational publishing is good experience but not my end goal'); and difficulty transitioning to industry or obtaining promotion in the workplace ('I'd like to move on to commissioning and team management' and 'I want to work in editorial but have so far been unable to transition').

### Students' Experiences Transitioning from University to Industry

As outlined in the introduction, the overall objective of this book is to investigate how effectively editing and publishing programmes prepare graduates for industry and how well these graduates translate this instruction to the workplace. Therefore, the first question to begin assessing this extent asked graduates to identify which of their university subjects prepared them most for working in the publishing industry; they were able to select more than one option from the subjects previously listed in Figure 5. The subjects that appeared to be most beneficial were copy-editing and proofreading (26 respondents, or 74%), structural editing, and print production and design (each with 17 respondents, or 49%), the contemporary publishing industry (13 respondents, or 37%) and the business of publishing and teaching press (each with 11 respondents, or 31%).

Given that 46 per cent of respondents had indicated earlier that they were involved in editorial work, the above findings are understandable. One respondent remarked that the 'Editing courses helped me to refine my technique as I practiced [sic] the art and craft in a structured, supportive environment'; and another stated that their training 'provided excellent grounding in terms of making us familiar with copy-editing, proofreading and structural editing, which made it easy for us to edit documents once we have familiarized [sic] ourselves with the house style we had to follow – no basic training was required at my workplace'. The least beneficial, and relatively most noteworthy, included freelance writing and editing (4 respondents, or 11%; see Figure 7). The reason why freelance writing and editing would be considered to be the least beneficial could be the time

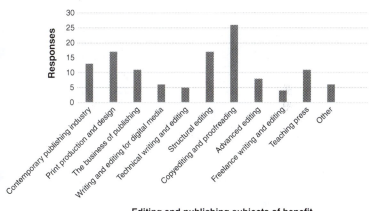

**Editing and publishing subjects of benefit**

Figure 7 The extent to which subjects benefited graduates[20]

required to build an editorial portfolio upon graduation. This is evidenced from previously supplied feedback: 'starting freelance with no experience for a CV is near impossible'. Other subjects that graduates identified as preparing them most for working in the publishing industry included desktop publishing (InDesign), ethical issues in publishing and media, ebook design, book marketing, 'national-level literary magazine' and 'annotation of academic writing . . . [and] indexing'.

Besides the units on copy-editing, proofreading and structural editing, the teaching press featured prominently in qualitative feedback with regard to editorial skills acquisition and industry perception. One respondent stated that working as a managing editor at their university press was 'hugely beneficial in developing my editorial skills'. These pertained not just to the conceptual and technical components of editorial work but also to the procedural and administrative:

[20] Student perceptions about the subject 'History of books and reading' (which was listed in Figure 5 on page 48) will be discussed at the end of this section on page 61.

As managing editor, I worked closely with authors throughout every stage of the editorial process, including developmental editing, copy-editing, and proofreading. For each stage, authors received extensive feedback on their book, and my job was to convey that feedback in a way that was authoritative, sympathetic, and supportive. Throughout the process, I learned how to effectively work with authors to turn each book into the best possible version of itself. This has helped immensely with my current job, where I provide editorial direction and feedback for my internal communications team. During the program [sic], I also learned to build and manage editorial calendars, which is a big part of my current employment. In addition, the editing classes I took (developmental editing and copy-editing) and the editing I did as managing editor helped me become a much, much stronger editor than I was at the beginning of the program.

A second respondent's feedback mirrored that of the graduate featured previously: with 'training at a teaching press, I learned effective project management and working with other teams to select, design, edit, market and sell a title'. A third respondent observed that participating in a teaching press appeared to replicate the real world, although very vaguely: 'Opening up your eyes to different aspects of the publishing industry' (while it would have been instructive if the respondent had explained the explicit nature of this 'opening', later feedback supplies relevant insight). In terms of the publishing industry more broadly, a fifth respondent explained that involvement in a teaching press was their employer's motivation for hiring them: 'The teaching press was mentioned by my boss as a specific reason I was hired for the internship and eventually career, because it gave me a base knowledge allowing me to be more efficient in my contributions'. Hence, experience gained from teaching presses is perceived favourably by both graduates and industry for their capacity to prepare graduates for the workplace and assist with recruitment.

One observation of respondents' qualitative feedback was how frequently words such as *basic* and *broad* were featured in relation to their university education; for example:

My publishing-related courses at university gave me a basic but broad understanding of editorial practices and how the publishing industry works . . . a basic knowledge of different book formats and binding types.

The teaching press . . . gave me a base knowledge allowing me to be more efficient in my contributions.

Learning the basics of typesetting and design also greatly helped with communicating with suppliers.

I was prepared on a basic level for editorial based tasks, copy editing and proofing . . . I also had a good understanding of the publishing industry which was good preparation.

I don't know if I was sufficiently prepared for the industry but given the basics to start. I learned on the job mostly and was completely unprepared for the pace of trade publishing.

Understanding the publishing industry in a broad sense and how all the cogs fit together. The challenges that the industry faces. Nothing specific to my specific role.

I was prepared with a broad knowledge of how the industry operates. However, I was not prepared for specific tasks in my job.

Therefore, respondents perceived they obtained 'basic' or 'broad' training at university, with at times little understanding of different book formats – which could, in turn, point to little awareness of different publishing sectors – and of the more particular, dynamic daily functioning of publishing houses. For instance, one respondent explained, as itemised directly above, that they were 'not prepared for the pace of trade publishing'. Though one respondent perceived this basic training to be advantageous for their current employment: 'I'm a member of a small publishing team with a bigger organization, so we all need to be generalists. The broad training I received prepared me perfectly'. In regard to acquiring practical experience before entering the publishing industry, one respondent indicated that the expectation as a student was that they 'enter internships or low level positions to get experience'. While the respondent did not identify the stakeholder group who expressed this expectation – universities or employers – this observation could suggest that some employers place more responsibility on universities to provide students with requisite practical skills, such as via teaching presses, rather than shouldering this themselves, as has been historically the case.

The more generalist nature of respondents' education at university was substantiated in their answers to the question about the ways, if any, they were not sufficiently prepared for employment in the publishing industry. Feedback related predominantly to:

- how respondents felt unprepared for negotiating digital content specifically and the digital, administrative aspects of publishing generally:

> Coding became a bigger part of my role than I first expected such as managing a website and doing research and development into digital publishing. We studied and created simple ebooks but I could have done with a more substantial introduction to it.

> Tactical considerations around metadata, title management systems, and distribution were not covered in any of my courses and were not prioritized [sic] highly at the learning press.

> Specific coding-related work used specifically by the company I'm employed by.

> We had no training in publishing software such as Biblio.

> I can't believe there was no in-depth training with MS Word. Like, yeah, we've all been using it for over a decade, but it is truly such a complex program [sic], and most people barely scratch the surface of its features and quirks just casually using it.

> Database training – there was a lot of content covered on Microsoft Word and InDesign especially, however using and interacting with data and spreadsheets was something I was underprepared for.

- how programmes gave scant attention to publishing roles and responsibilities outside the purview of book commissioning and copy-editing – that is, non-editorial roles such as sales and marketing, interdepartmental collaboration and human resources:

  > Permissions (or copyright in a comprehensive way); print production; book specs; liaising with printers; Ozalids & advances; contracts and author agreements; marketing & publicity; writing cover copy.

  > Dealing with designers Negotiating fees How to work with authors and communicate feedback Managing time.

  > We also didn't cover rights, sales, publicity or marketing in much detail.

  > [When] I had to work in the industry, I had to learn about components of publishing like book production, marketing, sales, and distribution, and how these affected my role as an editor.

  > There was no actual sales training really in the publishing program [sic]. Pricing a book is not selling it!

  > I was also not sufficiently prepared for understanding the human resources challenges the contemporary industry faces.

  > I was not prepared for any tasks other than editorial or a very broad understanding of the industry at large. I would recommend that publishing degrees prepare students for jobs other than editorial, e.g. sales, marketing, publicity.

- the lack of diversity when it comes to addressing the different publishing sectors, particularly educational and more technical publishing:

  > Technical writing Digital Media Medical & Scientific books/ journals Finance and Commerce.

We studied and created simple ebooks but I could have done with a more substantial introduction to it. I work mainly in digital publishing because of the niche part of adult education I work in.

I was not as prepared for structural/development editing in an educational publishing sense. Educational publishing was not the main focus of the course.

Digital publishing was not as thoroughly taught, specifically in how it applied to educational publishing.

I'm currently in comics which weren't covered at all and are very different from trade publishing in many ways.

Was unprepared to look for work in nontraditional publishing roles.

• how programmes insufficiently prepared graduates for freelancing:

I'm a freelancer, and I had little to no idea how to go about that. I also started out as a literary agent, and there was no training at all in that.

There was no preparation for freelancing, which needs to be a full class, including regarding taxes.

I did not feel at all equipped to be able to take on freelance proofreading or copy-editing work straight out of my degree.

• the broad nature of editing instruction, which then could impact adversely on how graduates approach unedited content and on communication with stakeholders, such as authors:

Needed more training on the grey/nuanced areas of editing (including subjectivity in assessment), and structural editing.

A greater focus on the copy-editing/proofreading aspects could have been provided. A few inclass [sic] activities and assignments over a twelve week period doesn't provide enough depth or variety to really tackle what is expected of you . . . Referencing styles was lacking and a major hole in my skill set. Legal subject could have spent more time on the intricacies of copyright law.

One major area I felt underprepared in was advanced grammar. Since I was not taught this kind of thing at school, and not much at university, I did not have the technical language to describe errors of grammar. I could recognise where something was wrong, but struggled to explain them succinctly.

While 'expectations', as mentioned earlier, could point to companies' placing more responsibility on universities sufficiently preparing graduates for industry, such as via internships and being involved in teaching presses, the majority of respondents (27 respondents, or 81.82%) indicated that their skills shortage was alleviated as a result of performing these tasks at their workplace – that is, on-the-job experience. For example, one respondent explained that 'I was trained on metadata and title management systems at work . . . I gained an understanding of how to navigate low compensation and inequity in book publishing through self-directed regional workshops, webinars, and online research'; and other respondents commented that 'Of course, every publisher does things a little different, and on-the-job training is an essential component to editorial education' and 'much of what my role entailed was learned on the job'. However, five respondents (or 15.15%) pursued other avenues to acquire requisite skills: independent and often web-based learning ('Anything I learned about freelancing and Word I learned on my own'), obtaining training through industry associations ('I paid for my own training with IPEd [The Institute of Professional Editors Limited] and the Australian Copyright Council'), and benefiting from more experienced colleagues and mentors ('I also asked editing colleagues to help fill in the gaps. I learned some other tasks at the publisher where I interned').

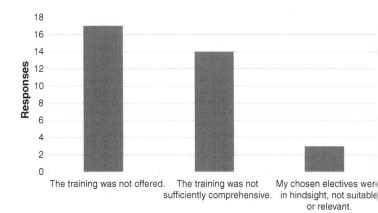

**Reasons for not receiving training**

Figure 8 Reasons for not receiving requisite training at university

Given that respondents had indicated earlier that the most beneficial subjects taught at universities were copy-editing and proofreading (74%), structural editing, and print production and design (49%), the contemporary publishing industry (37%) and the business of publishing and teaching press (each with 31%), the feedback enumerated previously confirms the suitability of university programmes' structure substantively, but that certain courses require greater specificity and specialisation; this is confirmed by Albers and Flanagan (2019, 9). Such conclusions were verified by respondents, as shown in Figure 8, in which the most common reason for not receiving the requisite industry training was that the training was not offered (17 respondents, or 60.71%), as well as by qualitative feedback: 'We only had basic classes in digital publishing because the programme's emphasis was still primarily on print'. Note, however, that three respondents (10.71%) stipulated that their skills shortage was related to their chosen electives not being relevant to their current employment, not the deficiency of the programme. Lack of sector diversity in programmes was also highlighted as a concern: 'Educational publishing as an industry was only touched on for a short week and not in depth'.

The online survey was concluded by asking respondents for their overall perspective – whether the publishing programmes at their universities sufficiently prepared them for industry. Respondents chose from a simple Likert scale of options: 'A great deal' (15 respondents, or 41.67%), 'A lot' (9 respondents, or 25%), 'A moderate amount' (7 respondents, or 19.44%), 'A little' (5 respondents, or 5%) and 'None at all' (0%). The respondents who selected 'A little' or 'None at all' were then required to provide reasons for their answers, most of which related to perceptions of relevance to the twenty-first-century digital environment and the immediate application of skills for that environment:

> I don't think they're all realistic. I think there needs to be more set subjects and less [sic] electives, because as wonderful and interesting as 'the history of books' was, it won't have an input into the majority of graduates' careers, unless they intend to move into academia. We also need ongoing technical training for production, e.g. typesetting, not just a one-off subject taken early and forgotten because the skills weren't continuously utilised.

> Publishing programs [sic] should focus more on the studio elements of publishing – editing, marketing and promotion, design, and digital – with hands-on work far more than the academic side, which is of limited value in terms of finding industry employment, particularly in the US. No offense to academics – what you do is commendable, useful, and necessary work, but besides building an academic base (which programs certainly should), ... academic work should be an optional track, not the focus.

> Most subject were far too theoretical for a degree intending to transition you straight into the workforce ... Digital and mixed media publishing was also lacking: editing for format neutrality, accessibility, etc. is crucial in the current industry. Legal subject was skewed more to media aspects rather than copyright, the core of a lot of income and legal issues in publishing.

> There was also an issue with the choice of instructors at times – a lot of them were working professionals using the

program to plug their own work, which seems like it could be fine but felt like it led to a very narrow take on the subjects. Some instructors were a mess as a result of their industry and personal struggles as well.

The more hands on experience is included in the program, the better off you are. The theory or history behind publishing is interesting, but doesn't really matter when it comes to working in the industry. The only 'history' that's relevant is understanding the market and how it changes.

It was observed in this book's introduction that a key challenge faced by educators of editing and publishing programmes since the late twentieth century is negotiating the tension between training students for current (and future), rapidly changing digital conditions and students learning the histories and long-standing principles that underpin contemporary publishing and print culture. This challenge is corroborated by respondents' feedback, particularly in relation to the perceived irrelevance of such courses as the history of the book and reading. Certainly, universities are not traditionally involved in the business of vocational skills acquisition but foremost the pursuit and dissemination of knowledge; by definition, they must deliver this knowledge to qualify as higher-education degrees. Universities provide students with the necessary framework within which to absorb and use the information and continue to do so after graduation, with the understanding that particular industry-specific training can be obtained elsewhere, such as on the job or via editing and publishing associations. However, for students to effectively appreciate today's 'history' and how this relates to 'the market and how it changes', as expressed previously by a respondent, they need to appreciate how the market has evolved in recent decades – indeed, over centuries. The publishing industry has a vibrant and rich history, dating back to Gutenberg and the first mass-produced books in the mid-fifteenth century. Educators hence need to challenge and inspire students to view as relevant all living histories for the ways they interrelate and influence one another.

## 4 Industry Perspectives

Three semi-structured interviews with an editor at Melbourne University Publishing (academic and scholarly monographs), two managing editors at Cambridge University Press (education and secondary and tertiary) and a publisher at Omnibus Books and imprint at Scholastic (trade and children's publishing) took place between January and February 2020, either face to face in Melbourne, Australia, or via conference call. All interviews were recorded, and material appearing in this book was approved by interviewees. The interviews are presented later as case studies to represent the major sectors of the publishing industry: academic, education and trade; however, each case study is organised according to this book's overriding themes: *being*, *learning* and *doing*.

As noted in the introduction, interviewing only Australian publishers does not conform to the international perspective taken for this book; nevertheless, it serves various important purposes: first, scant research has been undertaken for the Australian context; second, the three-month field-work period allocated for this project necessitated using my own local contacts to organise the interviews as effectively as possible; and third, the emerging COVID-19 pandemic required organising and conducting the interviews quickly. While the observations from Australian stakeholders are, by their nature, particular to Australia, they could be perceived to be applicable to international contexts because three of the four stakeholders interviewed are employed by international multinationals – Cambridge University Press and Scholastic.

The questions were related to the types of programmes from which employees graduated; whether these employees upon employment possessed the skills and/or confidence to complete their roles' daily responsibilities and to an acceptable standard; whether the publishing companies provided in-house training, or were employees required to obtain additional training elsewhere; whether the interviewees had relationships with academia in terms of providing guest lectures, accepting internships and/or acting as consultants; and whether they had assisted with, or provided advice for, developing, designing and/or revising university courses.

## *Melbourne University Publishing*

The book publishing branch of the University of Melbourne, Melbourne University Publishing (MUP), was founded in 1922 and is the oldest Australian university press, with other university presses being established more than ten years later: Western Australia in 1935, Queensland in 1948 and New South Wales in 1962 (Derricourt 2007, pp. 229–230). MUP is identified as the oldest Australian university press as the first university press to commence operation in Australia was Oxford University Press in 1908, with its office located in Melbourne (Thompson 2006, p. 329; Hargrave 2012, p. 238). Considered to be the pioneer of academic–trade 'crossover' publishing (Derricourt 2007, p. 229), MUP has published titles on subjects such as politics, history and current affairs; its first publication in 1923 was Myra Willard's *A History of the White Australia Policy until 1920* (Thompson 2006, p. 329). MUP's Miegunyah Press imprint has produced illustrated books relating to, for example, art, photography, history and biography, and its MUP Academic imprint has published Australian academic research and writing.

MUP's strategic direction radically altered in February 2019, with the decision to produce primarily academic titles (Muller 2019), unless specifically published under the Miegunyah Press imprint. The strategic changes also resulted in the appointment of a new eight-member editorial advisory board, all academics at the University of Melbourne: as reported in *Books + Publishing* (2019), 'MUP says the establishment of the editorial advisory board is in line with the publisher's "new focus on research and teaching strengths of the university"'. Prior to 2019, MUP published approximately fifty titles per year and expects to continue that level of output; indeed, in 2019, forty-eight books were published across all imprints, as well as four issues of *Meanjin* and thirteen reprints.

In February 2020, its editorial department comprised three in-house editors, one production manager and a publisher. In-house editors project manage numerous titles simultaneously and commission free-lance editors to complete the manuscript copyedit; substantive edits for academic books involve incorporating peer-review feedback and are carried out by authors, who are expected to work independently. Authors also organise their own permissions in terms of contacting copyright holders to obtain approval and invoicing. Although in-house staff do handle this for authors when it is determined easier to do so, especially when authors have little experience. Before the strategic change, the publisher conducted the substantive edits with authors, and once finished, the titles were passed to in-house editors to project manage until publication. Three sets of typeset pages are checked: the first two by the freelance editor and the third by the in-house editor; all corrections to pages are marked by hand on pages rather than electronically in PDFs. Though this preceded the lockdown in Melbourne from mid-August to October 2020 in response to the COVID-19 second-wave infections.

Two *learning* and *doing* issues emerging from the interview with MUP were industry perceptions of university postgraduate programmes, especially in relation to graduates securing employment in educational publishing, and internships.

## Industry Perceptions about *Learning*: University Postgraduate Programmes

The editor from MUP completed some years ago a part-time, two-year graduate diploma at a university in Melbourne while employed as a deputy editor of a literary magazine. For the first year, one unit involved examining the different genres of publishing, such as fiction, non-fiction and children's books, and each of these genres was taught by practising professionals; another unit addressed proofreading, such as pre-reading a text and the basics of grammar, spelling and syntax. For the second year, students undertook their main assessment, a group publishing project, where they role-played working for a publishing house, creating a list, compiling profit-and-loss sheets and so on. The MUP editor appreciated learning these aspects, such as profit-and-loss sheets, as they represented the daily practi-calities of many stakeholders in the publishing industry. However, as deputy editor of a literary magazine, such instruction 'sort of immediately disappeared' for its lack of immediate pertinence, though 'it was definitely good to know when you're talking in-house'. That is, this instruction enabled the MUP editor to be able to converse with her peers in an equitable manner – it indicated a common nomenclature and knowledge that promoted effective interdepartmental communication. Her overall assessment was that '[it] was nice to see different aspects of the trade and educational publishing and learn a bit more of the industry . . ., but it's an expensive way to do that'. In other words, most of the requisite skills for her immediate position at MUP were learnt on the job: 'Most of my job is communication with authors; a lot of my work is email. So really the people skills [are] something that you learn on the job and [weren't] part of any of the courses that I've done'. She admitted that the group project completed in her second year assisted with understanding how publishers work together, albeit these communication skills were not applicable until later in her career.

In terms of educational publishing, the MUP editor mentioned this publishing sector briefly when providing an overview of her graduate diploma in editing and publishing, though in the context of a professional editing trade and scholarly titles; therefore, the educational publishing sector was not relevant in a practical sense. However, when requested to suggest any improvements to the course that she completed, she explained that 'a lot of people that graduated from my course have ended up in education. There's a lot of jobs in education and . . . not that many jobs in trade'. The reason why there are more positions advertised for educational publishing in Melbourne is that most multinational educational publishers are headquartered here, including Pearson Education, Cengage Learning, Cambridge University Press and Oxford University Press. For the 2010–2015 period, 63 per cent of advertised educational publishing jobs were for Melbourne; in contrast, for Sydney, it was 27 per cent (Stegink 2015, p. 11). As Mackenzie (2011, p. 4) observed, 'Educational publishing accounts for about 40 per cent of all titles and many an editor relies on textbooks to put food on the table'. Consequently, the MUP editor believed it would have been instructive to teach more about educational publishing in her university course in Melbourne.

The word *aspirational* emerged in the interview regarding pedagogy and course design: for the MUP editor's course, '[It's] a little bit aspirational . . . it reflects back on the students . . .. What [students] want to do rather than what's likely'. This assessment was substantiated by graduates in the previous chapter: insufficient positions are available in their desired published sector, which necessitates obtaining employment in another, such as educational publishing, and that furthermore there are insufficient positions in the industry generally.

## *Doing*: Learning-by-Interning

MUP accepts unpaid interns, principally publishing and creative writing students, from postgraduate programmes such as at The University of Melbourne, which offers a semester-long internship unit as part of its master of publishing and communications degree. Interns are '[used at MUP] as a sort of backup . . . [as] another set of eyes' – ethical practice dictates that interns do not replace paid in-house employees. As related in the introduction, Florence (2013, p. 17) has observed the trend within industry to profit from unpaid internships: 'In a report from the Fair Work Ombudsman (FWO) earlier [in 2013], internships were found to be increasing in areas where there was high demand but few positions, including media, marketing, and PR, with evidence that "a growing number of businesses are choosing to engage unpaid interns to perform work that might otherwise be done by paid employees"'. The backup work at MUP involves shadowing, such as attending publishing and editorial meetings; completing editorial tasks, such as working on corrections and checking indexes; and undertaking picture research.

The overriding impression from this interview is that students generally approach their internships with an aspirational, romantic mindset – a conclusion that is corroborated by the managing editors at Cambridge University Press and the publisher/managing editor at Omnibus Books (refer to pages 68 and 75 respectively for these case studies). This is not unexpected, given that most students decide to train for a profession in the publishing industry because of a lifelong love of literature and reading, as identified in this book's introduction. This is additionally understandable because of students' theoretical knowledge of the industry only – put simply, they have yet to be employed in the industry to appreciate its myriad, interdependent dynamics. The outcome of this, however, is students' lack of awareness of the basic components of a book. As the editor from MUP observed: '[You] see someone [who's] decided to do Master's, but [they] haven't examined the book yet'. She offered the preliminaries as an example: 'Before you . . . ask questions . . ., look at a book and look at the imprint page, look at what's on the imprint page . . ., look at the half title'. Students' aspirational, romantic mindset therefore impeded their capacity – or perhaps their unwitting inclination – to view the 'book as an object' with specific commercial components.

## *Cambridge University Press, Australia*

Unfortunately, very little research into Cambridge University Press in Australia has been conducted. What is well acknowledged by the publisher and industry is that Cambridge University Press established an office in Melbourne in 1969, approximately sixty years after Oxford University Press opened its local office in Melbourne in 1908 (Hargrave 2012, p. 238). In a letter to the Australian Productivity Commission about the 'Parallel Importation of Books Study' on 17 April 2009, Executive Director Mark O'Neil (2009) provided Cambridge University Press's mission statement: 'Cambridge University Press, Australia and New Zealand (Cambridge) strives to serve the Australian Education market by publishing Primary, Secondary and Tertiary materials specifically designed to fit local curricula, local courses and meet local teacher and student needs. Cambridge University Press is a department of the University of Cambridge whose mission is to advance learning knowledge and research worldwide'.

Two managing editors – for academic and professional (A&P) and education – were interviewed for this project. The A&P managing editor admitted that her team was 'quite small': 'it's just me and I have a project editor who reports to me, and we report to the production [and editorial] director'. For education, this number was comparatively greater: the team comprised the managing editor and four project editors, all of whom reported also to the production and editorial director. In terms of personal history, the A&P managing editor had been employed at Cambridge University Press for more than sixteen years, initially starting as permissions coordinator and, a little more than one year later, promoted to the position of editor; she had been A&P managing editor for more than twelve years. For her university education (which bears relevance to discussion with the publisher/managing editor at Omnibus Books/Scholastic Australia next), she completed an undergraduate Arts degree, majoring in literature and classics. For postgraduate study, this managing editor completed a postgraduate certificate in editing and communication. The managing editor, education, completed a bachelor of communications, majoring in advertising, and afterwards a diploma in professional writing and editing. Workwise, this managing editor had been employed in the publishing industry for approximately twelve years: he 'started out manuscript assessing' for a vanity publisher; moved to an illustrated books publisher that specialised in such subject areas as architecture, art, photography and design and commenced employment at Cambridge University Press nine years ago as a project editor and was promoted to managing editor six years later.

Key issues resulting from the interview with the Cambridge University Press managing editors all relate to *being*, *learning* and *doing* (postgraduation): for *being*, expectations and background knowledge of applicants, including graduates, when applying for an editorial position in the educational publishing industry; for *learning*, suggested improvements to existing university editing and publishing programmes; and for *doing* (postgraduation), professional accreditation and the hiring of graduates.

## *Being*: Expectations and Background Knowledge of Graduates

When asked about graduates applying for editorial positions at Cambridge University Press and their expectations and knowledge, the A&P managing editor remarked somewhat wryly that 'we get on a lot of resumés that people have done creative writing and want to use their writing skills. And I'm like, that's not the job'. That is, graduates believed their knowledge about trade publishing and creative writing could be transposed into the academic and educational publishing sectors. Further afield, misconceptions related to what editors' work generally and how it was conducted in academic and educational publishing specifically. For example, the A&P managing editor had a primary teacher once apply for a position; when addressing the selection criteria, the teacher indicated that she could proofread because she had 'corrected students' work'; the managing editor in education contributed the following: 'People say I'm a good speller. I reckon I can be a good editor'. Another common misconception witnessed by the A&P managing editor related to distinguishing editorial boundaries between academic and educational publishing:

> I've had editors who worked on academic things and educa-
> tion things, and some of them can straddle both. They've
> been in education. They can come across to academic.
> We've had academic editors in the past who have been
> given education titles, and they're just can't [do the work].
> Thing is there's so much that they miss that they just don't
> even think to check. It is, I guess, such a different way of
> approaching content.

Such anecdotes implicitly point to earlier observations by the editor at MUP: graduates' misunderstanding of editorial responsibilities and tasks carried out in the educational publishing industry owing to insufficient coverage in university editing and publishing programmes. The A&P managing editor concurred that programmes tended to prioritise trade and literary publishing: 'It's a bit strange considering most of the industry, like most of the people coming out of those [programmes], will end up in an educational publisher in Melbourne'.

In terms of skill acquisition, the A&P managing editor admitted that she had conducted 'kitchen powwows' with Cambridge University Press editorial staff before the interview about whether their courses suitably prepared them for industry. The staff 'spoke highly of the structural and editorial English' courses at university; however, they confessed that besides developing an understanding of project management through group publishing projects, 'the rest of it wasn't really that useful once they had a job – it didn't actually help them with the [work] they were actually doing'.[21] One further significant observation about graduates'

---

[21] One such unit was the history of books and reading; the Cambridge University Press staff's mindset about not perceiving the relevance of publishing history to the modern context is consistent with graduates' responses to the online survey (see page 61).

knowledge was their lack of awareness of the specific components of books and the editorial tasks associated with them; according to the A&P managing editor: 'It's the elements of books . . . I think a lot of people across the board struggle with things like referencing, checking indexes, proof-checking, quality control [and] briefing freelancers'.

The Cambridge University Press managing editors therefore expected graduates would mostly learn requisite skills on the job; the A&P managing editor pointed out that 'so much of it doesn't makes sense until you start doing it. And then you're building your judgement and ability to do [work] better as you go'. However, supporting their graduate staff was made problematic by inadequate resources and time. The managing editor in education stated that 'we can never really spend quality, meaningful time with them . . . it always feels like it's a bit piecemeal. As something arises, you let them know because there's no sort of formal structure, education or induction'. Speaking about his own experiences when entering the publishing industry, he recounted quite nostalgically: 'You drown for a bit, but there is some satisfaction in discovering things for yourself or figuring things out for yourself as well'.

*Learning*: Suggestions for Improvement to University Programmes
When asked to provide advice about the types of knowledge they would prefer graduates to have learnt at universities, both managing editors were quick to respond and decisive. For the A&P managing editor, preferred knowledge pertained to book parts and digital work(flows):

> First of all, that would be production specs and things because I know I came in not knowing what things like bleeds were. And [it's] obviously not going to be a whole subject, but that sort of stuff it would be handy to at least have covered. And that would probably go for digital stuff as well, like basic info on digital formats [and] platforms. I know it's such a big area, but there are some key formats and key platforms that at least [graduates need to be] having some familiarity with. Even if you don't know the background stuff, . . . just how the content works, so that [relates to] referencing, indexing, imprint pages.

Reference to graduates' lack of knowledge about the basic components of books, such as imprint pages, and how they work interdependently as paratextual elements for the main body text is consistent among all industry professionals interviewed for this book. Similarly, for the managing editor in education, preferred knowledge related to digital and more specific technical work; however, he also signposted soft skills, such as time management and communication:

> I would say some training in basic design and maybe even some basic Photoshop training, definitely HTML coding . . . and more digital [work], background of coding with inter-active textbooks and also just general project management and time management and how to communicate. Yes, there's a lot of people [who] were sort of freaked out by the phone.

The observation by this managing editor about communication, such as answering telephone calls from internal or external stakeholders, is pertinent though industry stakeholders would most likely expect graduates to have little to no exposure to this administrative side of the business. Nevertheless, the managing editor's observation reveals a potential paucity of academic instruction for graduate students – that of management skills. This reflects the earlier findings of Greco (1990) and Baensch (2004), as detailed in this book's introduction, as well as that of Johanson (2006, p. 50), who included the following quote from a former colleague when addressing the difficulty of teaching editing to graduate students in her professional writing unit at Deakin University, Melbourne: '[A]bout 75% of the skills of an editor lie in her relationship with authors and other publishing staff, while the remaining 25% relate to the requirements of editing a text'.

## *Doing* Post-Graduation: Professional Accreditation and Hiring Graduates

Since being introduced in Australia in late 2008, a two-tier accreditation system has been administered by the IPEd. The decision to offer accred-itation emerged in response to, after 'many years', editors feeling 'the need to safeguard the status and standards of the profession' (Mackenzie 2011, p. 11). The first tier of accreditation involves editors completing a biennial four-hour, open-book, on-screen copy-editing examination, which 'measures competence rather than excellence'. The exam is open to anyone who wishes to complete it; however, the IPEd Accreditation Board recommends applicants have at least three years of full-time industry experience (IPEd 2020). According to Nixand Bean (2020, 4), who presented an overview of the accreditation exam for a meeting of Editors NSW (New South Wales) on 3 March 2020:

> The exam is onscreen in Word and PDF, which means it also tests [editors'] basic computer literacy skills – the ability to open and save documents on a computer, to navigate a digital document, to type and to select options – as well as [their] ability to use Word's Track Changes and Comments functions when editing. It does not test advanced Word skills, use of other Word tools or add-ins – although it does test [editors'] ability to refrain from relying on Spelling & Grammar check – nor does it test advanced skills in Acrobat.

Once successfully passed (a pass mark of at least 80 per cent is required), editors are afforded 'the [right] to use the words "IPEd Accredited Editor" in [their] professional profile, resume and marketing material (IPEd members may also use the IPEd logo' (IPEd 2020). The second tier of accreditation involves obtaining ongoing professional development. Accredited editors are required to renew their accreditation every five years (Nix and Bean 2020, p. 3), for which they need to demonstrate that they have 'been actively involved in the editing profession' and 'undertaken relevant professional development activities to maintain and extend their editing skills' (IPEd 2020).

According to Mackenzie (2011, p. 13), more than 250 editors sat for the accreditation exam in the first year, with more than 150 passing it; moreover, she observed that 'some companies and government departments now refuse to employ editors who are not accredited'. The impact of this decision by such companies and government departments is the potential marginalisation of graduates, who either may not have sufficient resources when commencing their professional careers, such as the funds to cover the registration fee – for 2020, the early-bird rate was A\$675 for IPEd members and A\$900 for non-members; the standard fees was A\$900 for members and A\$975 for non-members (Nix and Bean 2020, p. 10) – and/or have not yet had the opportunity to build their experience and portfolios, which certainly necessitates working in the industry for numerous years, often after developing a reputation among peers.

The A&P managing editor at Cambridge University Press is an accredited editor and renewed her accreditation 'a couple of years ago'. When the examination was first introduced, she 'wasn't that interested in it'; however, once encouraged by her production and editorial director and as she observed more editors completing it, she acceded, albeit admitting that '[it] was brutal' because of its difficulty:

> The first section was sort of general. [Questions were about] the legal requirements for CIP, an imprint page rather, and the nuts and bolts. And then there was an editing passage where you had to hard copy edit something and note queries and, you know, there's artwork and stuff involved in that. And then the third section was a sort of choose-your-own adventure depending on your specialty. So there was a trade section, a law section, a cookbook [section]. So you could answer questions about more specialised areas.

Nevertheless, the A&P managing editor recognised that accreditation was important for the professionalisation of editors in the industry generally and for creating opportunities for freelancers and retirees:

> [One] of my editors is pushing retirement age. She's been editing for a long time. [She asked] me last year if I could write her a reference for academic publishers in Canberra. It might have been a university one she'd been working with

for many years. But because they decided that they needed accreditation as a requirement to keep working or they needed recommendations, even though she'd been working for them for years, I [provide the reference]. I was happy to do it, but it was still very strange that that was their first kind of filter point, regardless of how long or how well someone had been working before that.

The managing editor in education, who had not at that time sat the exam himself, had previously discussed with the production and editorial director about his team completing it, though his project editors had communicated that they had found the prospect 'daunting' owing to the 'amount of work involved and the level of difficulty'. Therefore, for his team, sitting the accreditation examination remained an option, not a requirement. In regard to hiring in-house editors, both managing editors did not include accreditation 'as a basis for choosing people'. Hence, in the educational publishing industry at least, graduates are not penalised for having not passed the accreditation exam when applying for in-house editorial positions or freelance work – the latter more relies on reputation, networking and developing portfolios.

## *Omnibus Books/Scholastic Australia*

Established in Adelaide, South Australia, in 1981 by Sue Williams and Jane Covernton, the inaugural mission of Omnibus Books was to challenge the industry's systemic glass ceiling: 'We were two enthusiastic women, with a background in editing, art direction and production gleaned from several years at Rigby, who shared a hearty frustration with an industry dominated at the top by men, with women doing most of the work' (Covernton 2006, p. 299). They perceived their pooled abilities and resources to be especially suited to the niche, 'under-exploited' market of children's books at that time. Early successes included *One Woolly Wombat* (1982), written by Rod Trinca and illustrated by Kerry Argent, and *Possum Magic* (1983), by Mem Fox and Julie Vivas. The US multinational Scholastic, which opened its Scholastic Australia office in Sydney in 1968, acquired Omnibus Books in

1995 (Sheahan-Bright 2007, p. 297); Williams and Covernton departed Omnibus Books in 1997 to found Working Title Press (Covernton 2006, p. 300). According to Sheahan-Bright (2006, p. 302), Scholastic is 'the sixth biggest book publisher in Australia'.

With approximately thirty years' experience in the Australian publishing industry, the publisher/managing editor (though just termed *publisher* from this point) at Omnibus Books oversees the publication of children's fiction, non-fiction and picture books; she is also publishing manager of Scholastic Australia's digital publishing. Prior to this, and also at Scholastic Australia, she was employed as managing editor where she, among her numerous responsibilities, supervised the publishing of adult fiction and non-fiction, as well as children's picture books.

Two issues that emerged from the interview with the publisher at Omnibus Books both relate to *doing* (the second, post-graduation): learning-by-interning and graduates' difficulty discerning the boundaries of/between specific editorial labour, which impacted on their ability to conduct such labour.

## *Doing*: Learning-by-Interning

'Publishing is in such a weird place these days'. Interestingly, the publisher's wry observation preceded the upheaval caused by the COVID-19 pandemic to the Australian publishing industry from late March 2020 when most editorial labour completed previously on paper went digital, primarily in in-house and freelance editors' homes. This 'weird place' pertains to the industry's financial constraints and the reality that fewer people carry out greater amounts of work. For the period 2010–2015, Stegink (2015, p. 11) has observed that the 'fall in job ads over the past five years has been most pronounced in Editing, Sales and Bookselling. Between 2010 and 2011, the number of Editing job ads have halved, going from 141 jobs to just 70'. While receiving assistance from interns would therefore be 'a huge help', the publisher admitted that the policy at Scholastic Australia was to not accept interns: '[We] don't do that anymore because it's almost too much of an investment of time and money for the company'.[22] That is, Scholastic

---

[22] The trade publishing companies at which the publisher worked previously had identical policies.

Australia lacked the human resources necessary for daily editorial tasks to be completed alongside the supervision of interns: '[In] order for us to offer value to an intern, we have to have time. And with less people, more work, we don't have time to do the work in front of us'. In addition, and consistent with the editor at MUP, the publisher pointed to concerns about ethical practice: she personally was 'never thrilled about taking advantage of free labour'; however, she acknowledged that, without experience, securing employment in the current publishing market is extremely difficult – '[graduates] don't have anything'.

The publisher next explained that the graduate (or 'junior') editorial staff at Scholastic Australia were not expected to have completed internships as part of their editing and publishing studies before being employed at the company – it's not 'one of the things we look for'. Instead, to gauge their ability, graduates undertook a proofing/copy-editing test as part of their interview. The reason for this related to company culture and whether prospective employees were a suitable fit: '[It's] more about adaptability if they've got training. [You] want to know that they've had some training, whatever that is – whether it's in-house or whether it's [a] university course – and then it's just a matter of seeing how people fit'. Once employed, junior editors receive requisite mentoring from senior editors; this trend in trade publishing has been previously expressed by Anne Macpherson, head of Editorial and Production at Hachette: 'Our senior editors are responsible in part for guiding our junior editorial staff, passing of and mentoring work, and being available to lend a hand or discuss a project as required' (Lindsay 2016, p. 12). Though Macpherson conceded that Hachette 'also relied on external sources to provide suitable training in all areas of the editorial process'. One such external source identified by Lindsay was the IPEd.

Rather than completing industry internships, the publisher expected graduates who seek to become an editor of literary fiction to have been 'trained in English and literature' (note the use here of *trained*, not *educated*). That is, junior editors should attend to more than just editorial English aspects, such as punctuation – they need to engage appropriately with its content: '[That's] what helps me . . . that kind of understanding and love of story and character and theme and all those things. If I need to get some help at some point from . . . my staff or for editors with full stops or anything else or any other skills, we can get that'. The publisher's recommendation that aspiring fiction editors be trained in English and literature has previously been expressed by Robert Sessions (2013, p. 9), former publishing director of Penguin Books Australia when asked to offer advice for people interested in pursuing a career in publishing: 'Do a humanities degree at a good university; become active in student news-papers (or their equivalent); do [a university] course in editing and publishing . . . and use every contact you can in order to spend some time working in bookshop or at a magazine'. Contrary to the opinion of the publisher at Omnibus Books, Sessions also counsels 'doing an intern-ship at a publishing house'.

*Doing* Post-Graduation: Discerning Editorial Boundaries

Graduates' capacity to discern editorial boundaries was identified aptly by the publisher and, in the manner of most editors, succinctly using plain English: 'If someone wants to show off all their talents and abilities but doesn't do what they've been asked to do, it doesn't help them in the end'. That is, graduates often lack understanding of the 'demarcation of what a job is as an editor' – what editors do and/or not do and what each editorial task specifically entails. The publisher offered an anecdote as an example: '[Over] the years, if I have asked someone who's an editor to proof a book, they give me back something they've edited . . . I just need [them] to tell me the spelling mistakes'. When asked to suggest reasons for this trend among graduates, the publisher tentatively provided the following:

> I don't know if this has come from a gap in the courses or it's just aspirational thinking . . . But that's been a common problem I've had with people who have graduated more recently from whatever course they have come from – understanding the different roles . . . It could be just gen-erational and aspirational that they would rather do some-thing else. But it means that I really, really struggle to get someone who will just proof a book for me, regardless of all their abilities and talents . . .

The publisher's use of the word *aspirational* to describe graduates' mindset upon entering the publishing industry is consistent with what the editor at MUP observed earlier about student preferences and, in response, course pedagogy and design: '[It's] a little bit aspirational . . . it reflects back on the students . . . What [students] want to do rather than what's likely'. The aspiration of what is expected rather than what the situation is, or might be, in a publishing house in reality speaks to the generational aspect identified by the publisher; however, in this case, the expectations appear to originate from, and be communicated by, educators of university programmes, not graduates and their generation: 'a generational change of those people given expectations that weren't real, and they didn't give themselves these expectations – it's not their fault'.

Graduates' difficulty in discerning editorial boundaries in turn impacts on their performance of editorial tasks allocated to them. The publisher reflected that she had witnessed 'people get muddled in terms of their aspirations – [their aspirations] work against them'. She then provided an insightful example from her years of experience as 'muddled' evidence: 'I've had editors . . . completely remove the voice of fiction', as well as 'the pacing and all the quirks that make a wonderful fictional voice', in their quest to 'make all English perfect'. For circumstances such as this, the issues of concern are not just aspirations affecting their engagement with literary content and their respect of authorial voice but also ability appropriate for a specific publishing sector. According to the publisher, editors who tended to remove 'the voice of fiction' were potentially better suited to non-fiction editing: 'As a fiction editor, you've got to know [the rules of grammar] and then know if and when you have to bend them'.

To resolve graduates' aspiration muddling editorial performance, the publisher returned to the ideal 'training' suitable for fiction editors – English and literature:

> [If] someone is trained in English and literature, that is brilliant training because you spend years deconstructing literature. How does this voice work? What has this author done to create this character? Why do we see these

> characters' motivations? ... [In] fiction, if you are trained
> to ... understand how to build a character, you've seen by
> deconstructing it.

Those graduates, or junior editors, who remove the authorial voice, according to the publisher, are those who have bypassed studying literature as an undergraduate and moved directly to a postgraduate publishing and editing course. However, this publisher sought graduates who 'loved [reading fiction] and studied it'. This 'lifelong love of reading and intention to pursue a career in publishing as a result' aspiration, as discussed in this book's introduction, is different from the aspiration of 'expectation' identified directly above. It relates back to Einsohn's (2011a) question: 'Are editors born or made?' Are aspiring editors born with the necessary drive and aptitude to become competent editors and succeed in the publishing industry? Are drive and aptitude innate to the self, or can they also be formally cultivated? For this publisher, a successful fiction editor possesses both a lifelong commitment to fiction through reading and the requisite literary 'training' to engage appropriately with, and respect, content. Sessions (2013, p. 9) urged going one proactive step further: 'These days "liking books and reading" is no longer enough in itself! More than ever, you have to "make your own luck"'.

## 5 Conclusion

The objective of this book was to investigate how effectively university editing and publishing programmes prepared graduates for industry and how graduates translated this instruction to the workplace. As noted in the introduction, it is unrealistic to perceive universities as a one-stop shop for skills acquisition – this is not their purview, nor does the industry expect it to be. Nevertheless, professional education at universities is generally recognised as the necessary prerequisite, or gateway, for graduates to be considered likely candidates for employment. Put simply, '[w]hile it's not feasible to train students to know and do everything, we can prepare them to meet many industry needs' (Flanagan 2019, p. 40).

To gauge the effectiveness of university courses and graduate transition, this book adopted a mixed-methods approach of two online surveys for educators and graduates from universities in Australia, New Zealand, India, the United Kingdom, the United States of America, Canada, South Africa and Germany, as well as three semi-structured interviews with managing editors/publishers across diverse publishing sectors: academic, trade/children's publishing, academic and professional and educational publishing. Therefore, these stakeholders' observations serve to address the majority of the publishing industry. The mixed-methods approach therefore assisted with providing a more international, triangulated perspective – academic, student and practitioner – to appreciate publishing and editing education in the digital twenty-first century.

### *Key Observations Emerging from Fieldwork*

For educators, one-third of respondents had one to five years of experience working in the publishing industry; one-quarter had six to ten years; and two respondents, no experience. These educators' relatively modest to no experience is of concern and has been signposted earlier by Kruger (2007, p. 3): that a shortage of industry experience equates to insufficient understanding of the commercial, but also practical, realities of publishing. An outcome of this incognisance, as related in semi-structured interviews with managing editors/publishers, was graduates' persistent aspirational, romantic mindset that generally conflicted with modern publishing realities. More specifically, these industry practitioners believed that course design reflected more student expectations and/or aspirations than what students actually experienced when employed in industry. Canty and Watkinson (2012, p. 460) have also observed this:

> It could be argued that the emphasis of these courses reflects the interests of the students mostly aiming for trade publishing, but on the other hand these students often come to recognise during their study that most of the jobs are in academic, professional and other non-trade sectors.

Another outcome was graduates' perception of the 'basic' or 'broad' nature of university programmes; for example, that graduates had inadequate understanding of book components, such as prelims (copyright/imprint pages) and end matter (references and indexes) – industry practitioners interviewed concurred that this was a significant issue – and that their training left them unprepared for negotiating digital content specifically and for the digital, administrative aspects of publishing more generally: 'the skills employers now expect of [graduates] go far beyond classical editing. They expect some competencies in editing video, audio, [and] Web' (Lang and Palmer 2017, p. 298).

Educators with industry experience most commonly performed editorial and commissioning work; the least common types of work included production and marketing. In terms of research strengths, contemporary and historical print culture and digital and trade publishing were most prevalent, with the least being academic and educational publishing. These findings reflect graduate perceptions that scant attention is paid to diverse publishing roles and responsibilities besides book commissioning and copy-editing, such as sales and marketing, interdepartmental collaboration and human resources, which precluded graduates leaving with a whole-industry picture; that relatively little consideration is given to publishing sectors besides trade publishing, such as educational and more technical publishing; that insufficient guidance is provided for freelancing, which is pertinent as a substantial amount of work in industry is conducted by contracted staff to reduce or limit project costs; and that editing instruction often did not address how to communicate effectively with stakeholders, such as authors. This points to programmes' need to incorporate editorial dialogue in their instruction, as per Masse (1985, p. 36) – that is, instructing students on techniques that editors use to talk '*with*, not *at*, writers'.

While this book's focus is teaching editing and publishing, not sales and marketing, design or administration, a significant component of an editor's work not just pertains to correcting manuscript copy and typeset pages but also is highly administrative, conducted within complex, digital environments and requires frequent, if not daily, interdepartmental collaboration with myriad internal and external stakeholders (often offshore, with English as their second language). Therefore, being exposed to diverse roles and responsibilities besides book commissioning and copy-editing enables graduates to obtain a whole-industry perspective and equips them with the requisite vocabulary – or nomenclature (Fretz 2017), as outlined in this book's introduction – to effectively collaborate and communicate with colleagues and other staff. Indeed, a key research question posed by Albers and Flanagan (2019, p. 4) about 'current modern teaching methods' is: 'Is our definition of the editing course too narrow and should it include the broader functions a practicing [sic] editor is called upon to perform: document management, publishing management, coordinating revisions and reviews, etc.?' While pedagogy should not be obligated to cater to graduates' aspirations and/or expectations, feedback from this book's online graduate surveys – as well as understanding of the less-romantic practicality of editors' daily work, as enumerated previously – suggest that widening knowledge and practice of editing at universities would benefit both graduates and industry. According to Albers and Flanagan, these are also the 'nonword aspects of editing' that reside beyond the page, such as 'visuals, document usability, or information architecture' (p. 11).

In terms of pedagogy, all educators indicated that they applied a theory–practice synergy, either on or off campus (surveys were completed between December 2019 and February 2020 and therefore before the COVID-19 pandemic required the closure of universities and/or transition to wholly online delivery of lectures and tutorials from April 2020). Lectures were typically administered face to face, with practice-based group work – students' learning-by-doing – carried out in computer labs, studios, workshops and teaching presses (underpinned by collaborative ELT) and supported by online supplementary material and internships. Assessments combined traditional (written tests, practical exercises and projects) and online components (usually quizzes); most assessments were related to structural editing and copy-editing. Maintaining the traditional component of assessments, especially structural editing and copy-editing written assignments, appears somewhat misguided in the second decade of the twenty-first century when the majority of editorial work is performed and delivered in technical, digital environments; this conclusion is corroborated by Flanagan (2019, p. 36). Additionally, as communicated by Dunbar (2017, p. 307), written assignments embody an artificiality that is not representative of industry's reality: 'a consciously introduced variety of mistakes underprepares students to deal with the subtle and complicated error patterns that tend to appear over the course of lengthier manuscripts' (see also Melançon 2019, p. 180). This artificiality also hinders the collaborative, often organic work of knowledge workers – an endeavour that is embedded in commercial realities:

> A strict copy-editing course teaches editing equals 'make grammatically correct'. Of course, after editing, a document should have correct grammar, but if the overall document structure or content fails to communicate or fails to meet the users' needs, then the end result is a worthless, but grammatically perfect document. In other words, the company, the authors, and the editors have wasted their time and money. (Albers and Flanagan 2019, p. 5)

Although educators indicated that they had working relationships with myriad stakeholders in industry, this collaboration appeared to not flow meaningfully into developing pedagogy and curriculum. That is, most educators stated that they consulted with the publishing industry; however, the nature of specific industry involvement depended on time available (which educators tend to have little of) and amounted to the appointment of stakeholders to advisory boards and the hiring of sessional or adjunct staff, who most often were employed to teach – whose relevant practical insight and experience inform the delivery of content to students – but not contribute to developing pedagogy and curriculum. Other educators conceded that consultation with industry was more ad hoc and sporadic.

Regarding graduates, the most common sectors in which they found employment were trade and educational publishing; the least common were academic, magazines and self-publishing. This evidence therefore validates university programmes' need to attend to trade publishing in their curriculum, however not to the detriment of other sectors, such as educational publishing. This conclusion is corroborated by graduate qualitative feedback, interviews with industry practitioners and previous research: 'almost all . . . courses treat trade publishing as the norm and academic/professional publishing as "specialist"' (Canty and Watkinson 2012, p. 488). For graduates' specific work, editorial was most common, with the least common being production, design, commissioning/publishing, marketing and administration. While more than half of graduates indicated that they were employed in their preferred publishing sector, roughly one-third replied negatively and cited the following reasons: lack of advertised positions in their desired sector, lack of advertised positions in the publishing industry generally, lack of opportunities to gain promotion once employed and difficulty transitioning to industry.

Subjects from which graduates perceived they benefited the most were copy-editing and proofreading, structural editing and print production and design, followed by the contemporary publishing industry, the business of publishing and the teaching press. Other subjects that benefited students, as communicated in qualitative feedback, comprised desktop publishing (InDesign), ethical issues in publishing and media, ebook design, book marketing and indexing. The teaching press featured prominently for editorial skills acquisition, whole-industry understanding and hiring opportunities – employers appeared to look favourably on graduates with student-led teaching press experience. The least beneficial was freelance editing and writing; the reason for this was the fact that commencing a freelance career upon graduation with no experience was 'near possible'.

Overall, publishing and editing programmes were deemed sufficient by graduates; however, they admitted that they would have appreciated in hindsight more specificity and specialisation, as well as greater attention given to other publishing sectors besides trade, all of which have been identified previously. Albers and Flanagan (2019, p. 9) conceive a 'specialized [sic] editing course would be any advanced course that has a specific focus: web, usability, technology, management, or a different lens (as such as constructionism, feminism, and postmodernism)'. Many graduates additionally believed that courses should cater more for the twenty-first-century environment. Lang and Palmer (2017, p. 299) envision well this present – and future – reality:

> New multimedia technologies are bringing about a transformation in the way we communicate. As technologies for video production, digital animation, augmented reality, gaming, and media editing, become ever more sophisticated and widespread, a new ecosystem will take shape around these areas. We are literally developing a new vernacular, a new language, for communication.

Suggestions provided by graduates to mitigate this included having fewer electives and more set subjects; providing more technical training for production, such as typesetting; and focusing more on the studio elements of publishing – editing, marketing, design and digital – with greater hands-on technical work. Nevertheless, graduates alleviated their skills shortages through on-the-job training; seeking additional training elsewhere once employed, such as through industry associations – this could also be organised by their employer's human resources department (Canty and Watkinson 2012, p. 489); and being mentored by experienced colleagues and contacts.

For industry, key concerns related to graduates' aspirational misconceptions about the realities of the publishing industry: what was expected rather than what was, or might be, the case. For academic and professional, as well as educational publishing, misconceptions involved how knowledge of, and exposure to, trade publishing and/or creative writing could be regarded as transferable; misconceptions also related to the nature of the work and how the work should be performed. For trade, graduate misconceptions precluded their ability to discern editorial boundaries once employed – what editors do or not do; what each editorial task entails. This then impacted graduates' editorial performance, such as their engagement with content and respecting authorial voice. Albers and Flanagan (2019, p. 8) aptly, and perhaps wryly, observe that 'it's amazingly difficult to convince students to *edit* a text, rather than rewrite it'. Misconceptions also pertained to the editorial skills required for different types of content; for example, editorial skills necessary for fiction editing differ from those for non-fiction. Suggestions for improvement included providing more instruction on book parts, such as prelims, and digital work(flows); for soft skills, industry practitioners signposted time management and communication as being especially important.

## *Implementing Transition Pedagogy:* Being, Learning *and* Doing

It was acknowledged in this book's introduction that none of the scholars cited use the term *transition* when considering graduates' movement from academia to industry; the one approximating this was Chaffanjon (1994, p. 38), who used *transform* to articulate how the theory–practice–industry triumvirate empowers knowledge to become ability. This was also the case for educators when completing the online survey: the majority articulated their programmes' commitment to combining theory and practice as part of their pedagogy, the latter through collaborative group work, with students role-playing as apprentices, in computer workshops, studios and teaching presses to replicate real-world conditions and to assist with students acquiring the requisite and relevant practical skills to undertake work competently in industry. Words often used in surveys by educators were, for example, *collaborative, experiential learning* and *project-based*.

Certainly, students with the aspirations to pursue an editorial career most often start with rhetorical and textual understanding in place after experiencing a childhood reading literature and consolidating this by completing a humanities-based undergraduate degree (i.e. *being*). Though, as has been discussed in the introduction and supported by observations yielded from semi-structured interviews with industry practitioners, such background knowledge upon enrolling in postgraduate study does not necessarily lead to success in industry – both acquiring a position and being able to execute that position effectively. Universities are where students commence developing and/or reinforcing their editorial *being* and *learning* – that is, their editorial knowledge, attributes and nomenclature; and their practical skills – their *doing* – through theory–practice pedagogical synergy and learning-by-doing (such via teaching presses) and learning-by-interning (in industry). The recommendation here therefore is that educators weave transition pedagogy into their theory–practice pedagogy to address students' whole-of-university experience and beyond: the present and future requirements of their students in academia and industry. This means meeting as far as practicable industry expectations and being cognisant of market realities. In this way, *being*, *learning* and *doing* are the *transitioning* but interdependent concepts that, in unison, have the potential to form a holistic practice-led pedagogy for students of editing and publishing programmes.

# Appendix 1
## Educator Online Survey Questions

1  In which country do you currently teach?

   a  Australia
   b  Canada
   c  England
   d  India
   e  New Zealand
   f  Scotland
   g  South Africa
   h  United States of America
   i  Other (please specify):

   _____

2  For which position are you employed at your institution?

   a  Professor
   b  Associate Professor
   c  Assistant Professor
   d  Lecturer
   e  Assistant lecturer
   f  Teaching Associate
   g  Tutor
   h  Other (please specify):

   _____

3  Which of the following best describes your employment at your institution?

   a  Full time (continuing)
   b  Full time (on contract)
   c  Part time
   d  Casual
   e  Adjunct

h   Other (please specify):

_____

4   Have you previously been, or are still, employed in the publishing industry?

a   Yes
b   No (please proceed to Question 8)

5   If you answered 'Yes' to Question 4, in which industry are/were you employed before entering academia?

a   Trade (fiction, non-fiction, children's publishing, reference)
b   Education (primary, secondary, tertiary)
c   Academic (scholarly monographs and/or journals)
d   Magazines
e   Self-publishing
f   Other (please specify):

_____

6   If you answered 'Yes' to Question 4, how many years have/did you work in the publishing industry before entering academia?

a   1–5 years
b   6–10 years
c   11–15 years
d   16–20 years
e   More than 20 years

7   If you answered 'Yes' to Question 4, which type of work do/did you perform at in the publishing industry before entering academia?

a   Editorial
b   Commissioning/publishing
c   Production
d   Design
e   Typesetting
f   Sales and marketing

g  Other (please specify):

_____

8  Which of the following does your institution offer for editing and publishing students? (You can choose more than one option.)

a  Diploma and/or certificate
b  Graduate Diploma
c  Associate Degree
d  Bachelor of Arts
e  Master of Arts (coursework with minor thesis)
f  Master of Arts (research only)
g  Doctorate
h  Other (please specify):

_____

9  Which of the following describes your program's current research strengths? (You can choose more than one option.)

a  History of the book and reading
b  Contemporary print culture
c  Digital publishing
d  Trade publishing (fiction, non-fiction, children's publishing, reference)
e  Academic (scholarly monographs and/or journals)
f  Education (primary, secondary, tertiary)
g  Publishing and editing pedagogy
h  Design and production
i  Other (please specify):

_____

10  Please describe the pedagogy, both publishing and editorial, that underpins your program, including reference to design and administration of assessments. That is, how has traditional pedagogy changed or been amended by digital disruption?

_____

_____

_____

_____

_____

_____

_____

_____

11 Please describe your present cohort, in terms of enrolments for diplomas/certificates, graduate diplomas, and undergraduate and postgraduate degrees.

_____

_____

_____

_____

_____

_____

_____

12 For which of the following does your publishing program provide instruction? (You can choose more than one option.)

    a  History of books and reading
    b  Contemporary publishing industry
    c  Print production and design
    d  The business of contemporary publishing
    e  Writing and editing for digital media
    f  Technical writing and editing
    g  Structural editing
    h  Copy-editing and proofreading
    i  Advanced editing
    j  Freelance writing and editing
    k  Other (please specify):

_____

13 With which of the sectors of the publishing industry does your program have working relationships, in terms of guest lectures, internships and/or advisory consultations? (You can choose more than one option.)

   a Trade (fiction, non-fiction, children's publishing, reference)
   b Education (primary, secondary, tertiary)
   c Academic (scholarly monographs and/or journals)
   d Magazines
   e Self-publishing
   f Other (please specify):

   _____

14 Do you involve, or consult with, the publishing industry when specific units and/or courses are developed/designed and/or revised?

   a Yes (proceed to Question 16)
   b No

15 If you answered 'No' to Question 14, please explain your response.

   _____
   _____
   _____
   _____
   _____
   _____
   _____
   _____

16 If you answered 'Yes' to Question 14, please explain how you involved, or consulted with, the publishing industry to develop/design and/or revise specific units and/or courses.

   _____
   _____
   _____
   _____
   _____
   _____

_____

_____

17  Does your program operate a press?

   a  Yes (proceed to Question 19)
   b  No

18  If you answered 'No' to Question 17, which of the following reasons account for your program not running a press?

   a  In the process of establishing one
   b  Program too small to justify running a press
   c  Insufficient funds and/or resources
   d  Other (please specify):

   _____

19  Is your press student led?

   a  Yes
   b  No

20  Please describe the pedagogy that underpins the operation of your program's press. That is, does it reflect the course overall, or has it changed or been amended to teach the practice of publishing and editing?

   _____
   _____
   _____
   _____
   _____
   _____
   _____
   _____

21  Please outline the types of content your press publishes.

   _____
   _____
   _____

22 How does your press obtain and/or commission its content? (You can choose more than one option.)

    a  Unpublished authors (unsolicited)
    b  Researchers/scholars at your or other institutions
    c  Previously submitted student work
    d  Specific call for papers
    e  Other (please specify):

23 In which form do you publish content?

    a  Print only
    b  Digital only
    c  Both print and digital

24 Do you attribute the operation of your program's press to the success of your graduates in obtaining employment in the publishing (or related) industry?

    a  Yes
    b  No

25 Please explain your answer to Question 24.

# Appendix 2
## Graduate Online Survey Questions

1 To which of the following age ranges do you belong?

   a 18–22
   b 23–25
   c 26–28
   d 29–32
   e 33–35
   f 36–39
   g 40 or older
   h Prefer not to disclose

2 In which country do you currently reside?

   a Australia
   b Canada
   c England
   d India
   e New Zealand
   f Scotland
   g South Africa
   h United States of America
   i Other (please specify):
   _____

3 In which country did you complete your publishing (or related) education?

   a Australia
   b Canada
   c England
   d India
   e New Zealand
   f Scotland
   g South Africa

  h  United States of America
  i  Other (please specify):

_____

4  Please identify below the names of the undergraduate diplomas and/or degrees that you have completed.

_____

5  Do these undergraduate diplomas and/or degrees have relevance to the position you currently have in the publishing (or related) industry? If you select 'No', please explain your reason.

  a  Yes
  b  No (please explain):

_____

6  Please identify below the names of the graduate diplomas and/or degrees that you have completed.

_____

7  Do these graduate diplomas and/or degrees have relevance to the position you currently have in the publishing (or related) industry? If you select 'No', please explain your reason.

  a  Yes
  b  No (please explain):

_____

8  For which of the following areas did the publishing programs at your institutions provide training? (You can choose more than one option.)

  a  History of books and reading
  b  Contemporary publishing industry
  c  Print production and design
  d  The business of publishing
  e  Writing and editing for digital media
  f  Technical writing and editing
  g  Structural editing
  h  Copy-editing and proofreading
  i  Advanced editing

    j  Freelance writing and editing
    k  Other (please specify):

_____

9  In which sector of the publishing (or related) industry are you now employed?

    a  Trade (fiction, non-fiction, children's publishing, reference)
    b  Education (primary, secondary, tertiary)
    c  Academic (scholarly monographs and/or journals)
    d  Magazines
    e  Self-publishing
    f  Other (please specify):

_____

10  Is the sector in which you are now employed (as identified in Question 9) where you hoped to find employment after completing your education?

    a  Yes
    b  No (please explain):

_____

11  Which of the following types of employment best describes you?

    a  Full time (multinational publisher)
    b  Full time (independent publisher)
    c  Part time (multinational publisher)
    d  Part time (independent publisher)
    e  Casual (multinational publisher)
    f  Casual (independent publisher)
    g  Intern (multinational publisher)
    h  Intern (independent publisher)
    i  Self-employed
    j  Seeking employment
    k  Other (please specify):

_____

12 Which type of work do you currently perform at your workplace?

   a  Administration

   b  Editorial

   c  Commissioning/publishing

   d  Production

   e  Design

   f  Typesetting

   g  Permissions

   h  Other (please specify):

_____

13 Is the work you identified in Question 12 related to the position you seek to obtain as part of your overall career objective? If you select 'No', please explain your reason.

   a  Yes

   b  No (please explain):

_____

14 Of which of the following training provided by your institution's publishing program prepared you most for working in the publishing (or related) industry? (You can choose more than one option.)

   a  Contemporary publishing industry

   b  Print production and design

   c  The business of publishing

   d  Writing and editing for digital media

   e  Technical writing and editing

   f  Structural editing

   g  Copy-editing and proofreading

   h  Advanced editing

   i  Freelance writing and editing

   j  Other (please specify):

_____

15 Please explain below in more detail how the training you selected in Question 14 prepared you for working in the publishing (or related)

industry. For example, which specific editorial and/or publishing tasks were you sufficiently prepared for?

_____

_____

_____

_____

_____

_____

_____

_____

16  Please explain below in more detail in which ways, if any, the training you received at your institutions (as selected in Question 14) did not sufficiently prepare you for working in the publishing (or related) industry. For example, which specific editorial and/or publishing tasks were you not sufficiently prepared for?

_____

_____

_____

_____

_____

_____

_____

_____

17  Did you learn to perform these tasks at your workplace? If you answer 'No', please explain where you obtained this training.

a  Yes
b  No (please explain):

_____

18  Why did you not receive this training at your institutions? (You can choose more than one option.)

    a  The training was not offered.

    b  The training was not sufficiently comprehensive.

    c  My chosen electives were, in hindsight, not suitable or relevant.

    d  Other (please specify):

_____

19  Overall, did the publishing programs at your institutions sufficiently prepare you for industry?

    a  Highly agree

    b  Agree

    c  Neutral

    d  Disagree

    e  Highly disagree

20  If you answered 'Disagree' or 'Highly disagree' to Question 19, please explain, in your opinion, how these programs could be improved in future to better prepare students for working in industry.

_____
_____
_____
_____
_____
_____
_____
_____

# Appendix 3
## Semi-Structured Interview Questions with Industry Professionals

1 How long have you worked for this company?
2 Were you employed as a managing editor for this company, or were you promoted?
3 For which other companies have you been employed? How long were you employed there?
4 How long have you worked in the publishing industry overall?
5 Did you graduate from a university before commencing employment in the publishing industry?
6 If yes, from which university did you graduate and did it prepare you for the workplace? How, or not, exactly?
7 To what extent have you obtained on-the-job training? Have you obtained training elsewhere, such as at industry and/or society-convened workshops? Or a combination?
8 From which universities and/or programs have your employees graduated?
9 To what extent do you believe today's graduates are prepared by university publishing programs? More specifically, for which tasks/responsibilities do recent graduates have the necessary skills and confidence to complete to an acceptable standard?
10 For which tasks/responsibilities do recent graduates not have the necessary skills or confidence to complete to an acceptable standard? Why do you think this is the case?
11 Does your company provide in-house training? Do your employees obtain it elsewhere? If so, where? Or is it a combination of the two?
12 Do you have continued ties with academia, in terms of providing guest lectures, accepting internships and/or acting as a consultant?
13 Have you assisted with, or provided advice for, developing/designing and/or revising specific units and/or courses for academia? If so, what was the nature of this assistance/consultation?

# References

Albers, M. J. & Flanagan, S. (2019). Editing in the Modern Classroom: A Overview. In M. J. Albers & S. Flanagan, eds., *Editing in the Modern Classroom*. New York: Routledge, pp. 1–13.

Baensch, R. E. (2004). Education and Training for the Publishing Industry. *Publishing Research Quarterly*, 20, pp. 30–33.

Bridges, L. E. (2017). Flexible as Freedom? The Dynamics of Creative Industry Work and the Case Study of the Editor in Publishing. *New Media & Society*, 20, pp. 1303–1319.

Bunney, D. (2017). Facilitating the Transition to Postgraduate Studies: What Can We Learn from the First Year Experience? *Journal of Academic Language and Learning*, 11, pp. A23–A38.

Butcher, J., Drake, C. & Leach, M. (2006). *Butcher's Copy-editing: The Cambridge Handbook for Editors, Copy-editors and Proofreaders*, 4th ed. Cambridge: Cambridge University Press.

Butler, D., Coe, S., Field, R., McNamara, J., Kift, S. & Brown, C. (2017). Embodying Life-Long Learning: Transition and Capstone Experiences. *Oxford Review of Education*, 43, pp. 194–208.

Canty, N. & Watkinson, A. (2012). Career Development in Academic and Professional Publishing. In R. Campbell, E. Pentz & I. Borthwick, eds., *Academic and Professional Publishing*. Oxford: Chandos Publishing, pp. 457–470.

Chaffanjon, M. (1994). Industry-University Collaboration for Professional Education. *Publishing Research Quarterly*, 10, pp. 36–39.

Chavan, M., Bowden-Everson, J., Lundmark, E. & Zwar, J. (2014). Exploring the Drivers of Service Quality Perceptions in the Tertiary Education Sector: Comparing Domestic Australian and International Asian Students. *Journal of International Education in Business*, 7, pp. 150–180.

Cini, A. (2018). The Internship Experience. *Creative Net Speakers' Agency*, https://creativenetspeakers.com/internship-experience.

Ciofalo, A. (1988). *Establishing a Book Publishing Curriculum*. Maryland: Loyola College.

Clark, G. & Phillips, A. (2019). *Inside Book Publishing*, 5th ed. London: Routledge.

'copy editor, n.', OED Online, June 2020, Oxford University Press, www.oed.com/view/Entry/41299?redirectedFrom=copyeditor#eid8353803 (accessed 19 June 2020).

Covernton, J. (2006). Case-Study: Omnibus Books. In C. Munro & R. Sheahan-Bright, eds., *Paper Empires: A History of the Book in Australia, 1946–2005*. St Lucia: University of Queensland Press, pp. 299–302.

Crabbe, R. A. B. (2016). Training Opportunities for African Publishers. In K. Kamau & K. Mitambo, eds., *Coming of Age: Strides in African Publishing Essays in Honour of Dr Henry Chakava at 70*. Nairobi: East African Educational, pp. 236–255.

Derricourt, R. (2007). Book Publishing and the University Sector in Australia. In C. Munro & R. Sheahan-Bright, eds., *Making Books: Contemporary Australian Publishing*. St Lucia: University of Queensland Press, pp. 221–230.

Donoughue, P. (2007). Educational Publishing. In D. Carter & A. Galligan, eds., *Making Books: Contemporary Australian Publishing*. St Lucia: University of Queensland Press, pp. 209–220.

Donoughue, P. (2013). At War with the Future: The Publishing Industry and the Digital Revolution. In E. Stinson, ed., *By the Book? Contemporary Publishing in Australia*. Clayton: Monash University, pp. 15–21.

Dunbar, L. (2017). Using Real Manuscripts to Teach Professional Editing. *Teaching English in the Two-Year College*, 44, pp. 306–314.

Durack, K. T. (2013). Sweating Employment: Ethical and Legal Issues with Unpaid Student Internships. *College Composition and Communication*, 65, pp. 245–272.

'editor, n.', OED Online, June 2020, Oxford University Press, www.oed.com/ view/Entry/59553?rskey=dTzQ0r&result=1&isAdvanced=false#eid (accessed 19 June 2020).

Einsohn, A. (2004). Are Editors Born or Made? *Science*, 27, pp. 99–100.

Einsohn, A. (2011a). *Are Editors Born or Made?* UC Press, https://content .ucpress.edu/ancillaries/8429002/8429002_bornormade2.pdf.

Einsohn, A. (2011b). *The Copyeditor's Handbook: A Guide for Book Publishing and Corporate Communications*, 3rd ed. Berkeley: University of California Press.

Flanagan, S. (2019). The Current State of Technical Editing Research and the Open Questions. In M. J. Albers & S. Flanagan, eds., *Editing in the Modern Classroom*. New York: Routledge, pp. 15–46.

Florence, E. (2013). The Intern Experience. *Books + Publishing*, 93, p. 17.

Fretz, M. J. (2017). Speaking of Editing: The Nomenclature of Copy-editing. *Journal of Scholarly Publishing*, 48, pp. 243–267.

Geiser, E. A. (1997). Publishing Education. *Publishing Research Quarterly*, 13, pp. 110–117.

Gile, D. (1995). *Basic Concepts and Models for Interpreter and Translator Training*. Amsterdam: John Benjamins.

Greco, A. N. (1990). Teaching Publishing in the United States. *Book Research Quarterly*, 6, pp. 12–19.

Greenberg, S. L. (2015). *Editors Talk About Editing: Insights for Readers, Writers and Publishers*. New York: Peter Lang.

Greenberg, S. L. (2018). *A Poetics of Editing*. Cham: Palgrave Macmillan.

Hall, F. (2013). The Changing Role of the Editor: Editors Past, Present, and Future. In G. Harper, ed., *A Companion to Creative Writing*. Chichester: Wiley-Blackwell, pp. 179–194.

Hargrave, J. (2012). Disruptive Relationships: Past and Present State of Educational Publishing in Australia. *Publishing Research Quarterly*, 28, pp. 236–249.

Hargrave, J. (2014). Paperless Mark-Up: Editing Educational Texts in a Digital Environment. *Publishing Research Quarterly*, 30, pp. 212–222.

Hargrave, J. (2019). *The Evolution of Editorial Style in Early Modern England*. Cham: Palgrave Macmillan.

Harnum, B. (2001). The Characteristics of the Ideal Acquisition Editor [Article Dedicated to Ron Schoeffel, Editor-in-Chief at University of Toronto Press]. *Journal of Scholarly Publishing*, 32, pp. 182–186.

Haugen, D. (1990). Coming to Terms with Editing. *Research in the Teaching of English*, 24, pp. 322–333.

Hornschuch, H. (1972). *Orthotypographia*. *Historical Bibliography Series*, trans. by P. Gaskell & P. Bradford. Cambridge: Cambridge University Library.

IPEd 2020, 'IPEd Accreditation Exam', http://iped-editors.org/Accreditation/accreditation_exam.aspx (accessed 3 December 2020).

IPEd 2020, 'IPEd Accreditation Scheme', http://iped-editors.org/Accreditation.aspx (accessed 3 December 2020).

IPEd 2020, 'Renewal Requirements', http://iped-editors.org/Accreditation/Renewal_of_accreditation/Guidelines_for_renewal.aspx (accessed 3 December 2020).

Johanson, K. (2006). Dead, Done for and Dangerous: Teaching Editing Students What Not to Do. *New Writing: The International Journal for the Practice and Theory of Creative Writing*, 3, pp. 47–55.

Johnson, I. M. & Royle, J. M. (2000). Education and Training for Publishing in Britain Prepares for the 'Information Society'. *Publishing Research Quarterly*, 16, pp. 10–28.

Kerlen, D. (2001). Publishing Training and Buchwissenschaft in Germany. *Publishing Research Quarterly*, 16, pp. 23–27.

Kift, S. (2015). A Decade of Transition Pedagogy: A Quantum Leap in Conceptualising the First Year Experience. *HERDSA Review of Higher Education*, 2, pp. 51–86.

Kift, S. & Nelson, K. (2005). Beyond Curriculum Reform: Embedding the Transition Experience. HERDSA Conference 2005, University of Sydney, pp. 225–235.

Kolb, A. Y. & Kolb, D. A. (2005). Learning Styles and Learning Spaces: Enhancing Experiential Learning in Higher Education. *Academy of Management Learning & Education*, 4, pp. 193–212.

Kolb, A. Y. & Kolb, D. A. (2009). Experiential Learning Theory: A Dynamic, Holistic Approach to Management Learning, Education and Development. In S. J. Armstrong & C. V. Fukami, eds., *The SAGE Handbook of Management Learning, Education and Development*. London: Sage, pp. 42–68.

Kruger, H. (2007). Training Text Editors as Part of a General Programme in Language Practice: A Process-Oriented Approach. *Southern African Linguistics and Applied Language Studies*, 25, pp. 1–16.

Laham, N. (1990). Teaching Publishing in France. *Book Research Quarterly*, 6, pp. 20–25.

Lang, S. & Palmer, L. (2017). Reconceiving Technical Editing Competencies for the 21st Century: Reconciling Employer Needs with Curricular Mandates. *Technical Communication*, 64, pp. 297–309.

Law, M. A. & Kruger, H. (2008). Towards the Professionalisation of Editing in South Africa. *Southern African Linguistics and Applied Language Studies*, 26, pp. 479–493.

Lee, K. (2019). What's Important About Editors? *Books + Publishing*, 98, pp. 16–17.

Lindsay, P. (2016). Smarten Up. *Books + Publishing*, 95, pp. 11–13.

Mackenzie, J. (2011). *The Editor's Companion*, 2nd ed. Port Melbourne: Cambridge University Press.

Masse, R. E. (1985). Theory and Practice of Editing Processes in Technical Communication. *IEEE Transactions on Professional Communication*, pp. 34–42.

Maxwell, J. (2014). Publishing Education in the 21st Century and the Role of the University. *Journal of Electronic Publishing*, 17, http://doi.org/ 10.3998/3336451.0017.205.

McNamara, J., Field, R., Coe, S., Butler, D., Brown, C. & Kift, S. (2015). Capstones as Transitional Experiences. *Legal Education Review*, 25, pp. 7–28.

Melonçon, L. (2019). A Field-Wide View of Undergraduate and Graduate Editing Courses in Technical and Professional Communication Programs. In M. J. Albers & S. Flanagan, eds., *Editing in the Modern Classroom*. New York: Routledge, pp. 171–191.

Montagnes, I. (1997). Education for Publishing: The Needs of the Global South. *Journal of Scholarly Publishing*, 28, pp. 246–256.

Moxon, J. (1683). *Mechanick Exercises or, the Doctrine of Handy-Works. Applied to the Art of Printing*, vol 2. London: Printed for Joseph Moxon.

Muller, L. (2019). Say Goodbye to Melbourne University Publishing As We Know It. *The Sydney Morning Herald*, www.smh.com.au/entertain ment/books/say-goodbye-to-melbourne-university-publishing-as-we-know-it-20190206-p50w48.html.

MUP Appoints New Directors, Editorial Advisory Board (2019). *Books + Publishing*, www.booksandpublishing.com.au/?s=accreditation&x= 4&y=10.

Nix, L. & Bean, J. (2020). Accreditation Exam 2020: An Overview. *Institude of Professional Editors (IPEd)*, http://iped-editors.org/site/ DefaultSite/filesystem/documents/Accreditation%202020/Overview% 202020%20accreditation%20exam.pdf.

O'Donnell, M. (2015). Curriculum Narratives: Learning as Transition, Transition as Learning. *STARS: Students Transitions Achievement Retention & Success*, Melbourne, pp. 1–5.

O'Donnell, M., Wallace, M., Melano, A., Lawson, R. & Leinonen, E. (2015). Putting Transition at the Centre of Whole-of-Curriculum Transformation. *Student Success*, 6, pp. 73–79.

O'Neil, M. (2009). RE: Parallel Importation of Books Study. *To Australian Productivity Commission*, www.pc.gov.au/inquiries/completed/books/submissions/subdr445.pdf.

O'Shaughnessy, T., Michael, R. & Scott, R. (2019). From Cultural Entrepreneurs to an Apprenticeship Practice. In M. Weber & A. Mannion, eds., *Book Publishing in Australia: A Living Legacy*. Clayton: Monash University, pp. 29–51.

Osborne, G. (2009). How Did I Get Here? *Bookseller + Publisher Magazine*, 88, p. 14, https://search.informit.org/doi/10.3316/INFORMIT.675383030219006.

Poland, L. (2007). The Business, Craft and Profession of the Book Editor. In D. Carter & A. Galligan, eds., *Making Books: Contemporary Australian Publishing*. St Lucia: University of Queensland Press, pp. 96–115.

PWC, *Books*, https://www.pwc.com.au/industry/entertainment-and-media-trends-analysis/outlook/2020/consumer-and-educational-books/data.html (accessed 7 December 2021).

Schultz, M. (2019). Pay to Play: Internships, Post-Graduate Education, and the Cost of Working in Publishing. *Book Publishing Final Research Paper*, p. 39, https://pdxscholar.library.pdx.edu/eng_bookpubpaper/39.

Sessions, R. (2013). Farewell to the Book Trade. *Books + Publishing*, 93, p. 9, www.booksandpublishing.com.au/newsletter/wbn/2013/10/16/.

Shade, L. R. & Jacobsen, J. (2015). Hungry for the Job: Gender, Unpaid Internships, and the Creative Industries. *The Sociological Review*, 63:S1, pp. 188–205.

Sheahan-Bright, R. (2006). Case-Study: Scholastic Australia. In C. Munro & T. Sheahan-Bright, eds., *Paper Empires: A History of the Book in*

*Australia, 1946–2005*. St Lucia: University of Queensland Press, pp. 302–307.

Sheahan-Bright, R. (2007). Supermarket: Australian Children's Publishing. In D. Carter & A. Galligan, eds., *Making Books: Contemporary Australian Publishing*. St Lucia: University of Queensland Press, pp. 286–304.

Sides, C. & Mrvica, A. (2017). *Internships: Theory and Practice*. Milton Park, Oxon: Routledge.

Siebert, L. (n.d.). Supporting Media and Publishing Internships. *Hardie Grant Media*, www.hardiegrant.com/au/media/blog/supporting-media-and-publishing-internships.

Stegink, V. (2015). Publishing Job Ads in Decline. *Books + Publishing*, 95, pp. 10–11, https://search.informit.org/doi/10.3316/INFORMIT.367166829058562.

Targ, W. (1985). What Is an Editor? In G. Gross, ed., *Editors on Editing*. New York: Harper & Row, pp. 3–32.

Thompson, F. (2006). Case-Study: University Presses. In C. Munro & R. Sheahan-Bright, eds., *Paper Empires: A History of the Book in Australia, 1946–2005*. St Lucia: University of Queensland Press, pp. 328–336.

Upton, P. & Maner, R. (1997). Nature versus Nurture in the Making of a Manuscript Editor. *Journal of Scholarly Publishing*, 28, https://search.proquest.com/docview/213893689?accountid=12528.

Watkins, R. (2013). Eating, Breathing & Talking Books. *Books + Publishing*, 93, p. 11, www.booksandpublishing.com.au/articles/2013/07/15/27732/eating-breathing-talking-books-profile-on-robert-watkins/.

Woodings, R. (1990). Teaching Publishing in the United Kingdom. *Book Research Quarterly*, 6, pp. 6–11.

# Acknowledgements

The publication of this book would not have been possible without the assistance and support of many. Sincerest thanks to Dr Susan Greenberg (University of Roehampton), a coordinating editor of this 'Editing' strand, for her guidance when developing this project, her much-appreciated patience in its writing during the challenging COVID years of 2020–2021 and her insightful critical and editorial eye when providing feedback. To Katherine Day (University of Melbourne), for reviewing early versions of the educator and graduate online surveys and providing excellent feedback before distribution. To the many educators contacted in November– December 2019 at the following universities for distributing the surveys among colleagues and graduates: University of Melbourne and Curtin University, Australia; Whitireia Community Polytechnic, New Zealand; Jadavpur University, India; Stirling University and Oxford Brookes University, United Kingdom; Portland State University, United States of America; Simon Fraser University and Ryerson University, Canada; University of Pretoria, South Africa; and University of Münster, Germany. To all the graduates contacted through university alumna Facebook sites for completing the surveys. To the managing editors at Cambridge University Press, Australia, and Melbourne University Publishing and the publisher/managing editor at Omnibus Books, an imprint of Scholastic Australia, for volunteering their time to be interviewed in January– February 2020. To the School of Culture and Communication, University of Melbourne, for providing funds through the Sessional Research Grant to cover fieldwork costs in 2019–2020. And, finally, to my family – my husband Stuart, who generously donated his weekends to assist with transcribing interviews, and my children Eloise and Luke – for their unconditional love and support: they not only understand my enduring love for all things editorial and publishing but also provide the structure and love that enable me to pursue it.

**Cambridge Elements** ☰

# Publishing and Book Culture

SERIES EDITOR
## Samantha Rayner
*University College London*

Samantha Rayner is a professor of publishing and book cultures at UCL. She is also a director of UCL's Centre for Publishing, co-director of the Bloomsbury CHAPTER (Communication History, Authorship, Publishing, Textual Editing and Reading) and co-chair of the Bookselling Research Network.

ASSOCIATE EDITOR
## Leah Tether
*University of Bristol*

Leah Tether is a professor of medieval literature and publishing at the University of Bristol. With an academic background in medieval French and English literature and a professional background in trade publishing, Leah has combined her expertise and developed an international research profile in book and publishing history from manuscript to digital.

## ABOUT THE SERIES

This series aims to fill the demand for easily accessible, quality texts available for teaching and research in the diverse and dynamic fields of publishing and book culture. Rigorously researched and peer-reviewed Elements will be published under themes, or 'Gatherings'. These Elements should be the first check point for researchers or students working on that area of publishing and book trade history and practice: we hope that situated so logically at Cambridge University Press, where academic publishing in the United Kingdom began, it will develop to create an unrivalled space where these histories and practices can be investigated and preserved.

**Cambridge Elements** ☰

# Publishing and Book Culture

*Editors and Editing*

## Gathering Editor: Susan Greenberg

Susan Greenberg is a senior lecturer in the University of Roehampton's School of Humanities and Social Sciences. She is also a convener of the MA Publishing and Publisher of the School's in-house imprint, Fincham Press. Her last book, *A Poetics of Editing* (2018), makes a case for a new field of Editing Studies.

---

### ELEMENTS IN THE GATHERING

A full series listing is available at: www.cambridge.org/EPBC

Printed in the United States
by Baker & Taylor Publisher Services